WILLIAMS-SONOMA

Fish for dinner

WELDON OWEN

Contents

Understanding Fish

When choosing seafood, you may be inspired by a particular recipe, or by something that appeals to you at the market. Either approach is fine, but when in doubt, ask your fishmonger for help.

Fish Fillets

Fish fillets are the most convenient cut for everyday cooking. To yield a fillet, all the flesh from one side of the fish is removed in a single piece. A single fillet of a medium-sized fish makes enough for a single serving. Larger fish will yield several portions from each fillet, while it may take two or more fillets of very small fish to equal one serving. Eating fillets with the skin still attached is a matter of preference, but you can easily remove the skin either before cooking (page 124) or after. If you don't want to remove the skin from the fish yourself, ask your fishmonger, who will be happy to do it for you.

Fish Steaks

Larger, densely muscled fish are often sold as steaks, that is, crosscut pieces that may or may not include skin and bones. A salmon steak is simply a crosscut of the whole fish, while whole swordfish, tuna, and halibut are typically halved or quartered before being cut into steaks.

Whole Fish

Some markets display their fish whole and then either sell them intact, or cut them into fillets or steaks to order. This has several advantages: the skin protects the flesh from drying out and from bacteria, and the bones

help the flesh keep its shape. The skin and bones will also moderate heat for more even cooking and increase moisture.

Shellfish

For all their variety, shellfish can be easily grouped into two broad categories: crustaceans and mollusks. Crustaceans feature a tough external skeleton and move around using their appendages or small fins. Crabs, lobsters, and shrimp are in this group. Mollusks include bivalves, shellfish that live within two hinged shell halves, such as oysters, clams and mussels; and cephalopods, whose shells are actually quill-like pieces of cartilage within their bodies, like squid. Many types of shellfish are sold live, protecting their flavor and texture.

Storing Fish & Shellfish

Refrigerate seafood purchases as quickly as possible, ideally on a shallow pan of ice in their original wrapping. Store them in the coldest part of the refrigerator, typically near the back. Live shellfish, such as clams or mussels, should be stored in a bowl covered with a damp cloth, never tightly wrapped or sitting in water. Shrimp can be stored in a resealable plastic bag. All seafood should be used either the same day of purchase or within one day to ensure the freshest flavor.

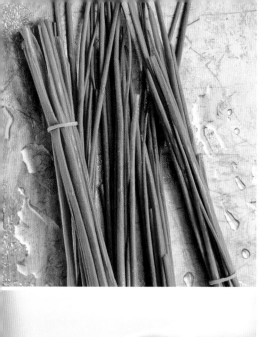

Flavoring & Seasoning

The flavors and textures of fish and shellfish are complemented by a wide variety of seasonings and sauces, from smoky chipotle to buttery hollandaise to bright, fragrant citrus.

Salt & Other Seasonings

As with most foods, salt is the basic seasoning for seafood. The recipes in this book call for kosher salt, which consists of coarse, flaky crystals. If using regular table salt, start with half the amount called for in the recipe and then adjust it to taste. It's a good idea to use freshly ground black or white pepper to season fish or shellfish. It's flavor is far superior to that of the pre-ground spice.

Herbs & Spices

The recipes in this book generally call for fresh herbs, whose bright, verdant flavor is the perfect fit with sea-fresh fish. When a recipe does call for dried herbs or spices, make sure that they have been recently purchased and are still aromatic. If they are older than six months, refresh your supply.

Sauces

Sauces for seafood can be as simple a squeeze of lemon and a scattering of fresh herbs on halibut fillets, or as elaborate as a rich, creamy egg-and-butter hollandaise over poached salmon. The key to pairing sauces with fish is to enhance, never mask, the flavor and texture of the seafood. Dipping sauces, such as an Asian-inspired combination of soy sauce spiked with ginger, or simply melted butter with fresh herbs are delicious options.

Pan sauces made with the drippings left in the sauté or roasting pan make use of the flavorful browned bits left after cooking fish or shellfish. Simple egg emulsions, such as mayonnaise or garlicky aioli, are also classic accompaniments to all types of fish.

Glazes

Somewhere between a marinade and a sauce, a glaze is a liquid mixture that, when exposed to the direct heat of a broiler or grill, caramelizes and forms a flavorful surface on the fish. Glazes, which often include flavorful ingredients such as sweet miso, chipotle peppers, or honey-mustard, are usually best for meaty, firm-fleshed fish, such as tuna or salmon, which can stand up to stronger flavors.

Coatings & Crusts

Delicate fish and shellfish also provide delicious opportunities for dishes that have a pleasing contrast of textures. Using a crust or coating helps seal the flavorful juices in and keeps fish or shellfish from drying out. For example, deep-frying tender fish fillets in a light batter gives it a crisp crust and keeps the fish moist. A layer of bread crumbs, chopped nuts, or even ground spices makes a light coating with some crunch when sautéing, roasting, or grilling.

SHOPPING FOR FISH AND SHELLFISH

A good fish market will clearly identify its products, where they came from, and how they were harvested and stored. Ask questions; if the answers are vague, consider shopping elsewhere. Fresh seafood is ideal, but it's not practical to ship some types, especially shrimp and squid, fresh across long distances, so they are routinely frozen.

Fish should be displayed chilled, preferably on a bed of ice, and, whether whole or cut into pieces, it should glisten. Dull colors and dry surfaces are warning signs. The darker flesh on the skinned side of fish fillets should be reddish, not brown. Also, trust your nose. No fish market is going to smell like a rose garden, but avoid places with a strong fishy smell.

When choosing mussels, clams, and oysters, look for those that are tightly closed, or that close when disturbed. Live crabs should be very active. Shrimp should be spot free and even in color, except for striped varieties. Choose squid with clear skin neatly dotted with black, rather than splotches of pink or purple.

Seafood spoils quickly, so keeping it cold is essential. If you cannot get seafood home quickly, bring along a cooler or have it packed in ice.

Fish's delicate, sweet flesh becomes deliciously charred on a hot

grill. Shellfish, too, are excellent when grilled, gaining an appealing

smoky flavor after cooking. The following recipes can be made

on either a charcoal or gas grill, whichever you have on hand in

Grilled & Broiled

the backyard. Step-by-step instructions for setting up these

grills for cooking can be found on pages 134–35. Or, make one

of the mouthwatering broiled recipes in this chapter. Broiling

utilizes a high heat that mimics that of an outdoor grill to produce

caramelized glazes that deliciously coat the fish.

Fish Types for Grilling

Firm-fleshed fish, thickly cut, work best on the grill or under the broiler. Choose tuna, salmon, swordfish, halibut, snapper, mahimahi, or a similar fish. Shrimp and scallops, with their firm, but buttery flesh, also work well. Delicate fish, such as sole, is tricky to grill, often better suited for sautéing or panfrying (page 34).

Preparing to Grill or Broil

Trim off any excess skin from fish fillets or steaks and remove any pin bones (page 124). Oil the grill rack and/or the fish well before grilling to prevent it from sticking to the grill grate. When grilling fish, it is important to thoroughly scrub the grate with a wire brush before cooking to ensure that the fish doesn't stick to the grill.

Using an Indoor Grill

In theory, indoor electric grills and grill pans can be used in the same way as outdoor grills, but because they don't include a cover, their use is limited to direct-heat cooking. The timing may be longer than is indicated in the recipe, as these grills generally do not get as hot as outdoor gas grills. Be sure to follow the recipe's doneness cues.

Tips & Tricks

Broiling Fish

The same cuts that work on the grill are suitable for broiling. For best results, preheat the broiler for about 15 minutes before cooking. Before you start, position the oven rack about 3 inches (7.5 cm) away from the heat source to ensure even cooking. Turn on your oven light so you can check on the cooking progress without opening the oven door.

Creating Grill Marks

To give your fish professional-looking grill marks, after one-fourth of the total cooking time has elapsed, use a spatula or tongs to rotate each piece of fish 90 degrees and place back on a different spot on the grill rack. Continue to cook until the halfway point. Turn the fish over and repeat the process on the other side, turning the fish 90 degrees at the halfway point.

Gauging the Heat

If you are using a charcoal grill, or if your gas grill does not have a built-in thermometer, hold your hand about 4 inches (10 cm) above the grill rack after the grill has preheated. Keep your hand in the same position as long as you comfortably can and count. Medium-high heat corresponds to 2 or 3 seconds; medium heat is reached when you can count 3 or 4 seconds.

Cooking the shellfish on one set of skewers and the vegetables on another ensures perfect doneness for both. Grilling over an open fire accentuates the sweetness of the shellfish and vegetables.

Shellfish & Vegetable Skewers

- Soak 12 wooden skewers in water to cover; set aside. In a small bowl, combine the garlic, thyme, bay leaves, a pinch of pepper, and the oil and set aside.

- Thread a shrimp onto a skewer so that it forms a C-shape. Thread a scallop horizontally onto the skewer. Repeat to add one more shrimp and one more scallop onto the skewer. Assemble 5 additional skewers in the same manner. Lay the skewers in a shallow dish and drizzle with about 2 tablespoons of the flavored oil. Squeeze the lemon half over all and turn to coat evenly.

- Thread alternating pieces of the vegetables onto the remaining 6 skewers. Lay the finished skewers in a shallow dish, season with ¼ teaspoon salt and a pinch of pepper, and brush with about half of the remaining flavored oil.

- Prepare a grill for direct-heat cooking over medium-high heat (page 134). When the grill is hot, lightly brush the grill rack with canola oil. Lay the skewers across the hottest part of the fire. Cook, turning once, until the shrimp are opaque throughout and the scallops show dark brown grill marks (it's fine if the scallops are slightly translucent in the centers), about 3 minutes per side. Cook the vegetables until the zucchini is tender and nicely marked with medium brown grill marks, about 3 minutes per side.

- Transfer to a platter, brush the vegetables with the remaining flavored oil, and serve right away.

2 cloves garlic, crushed

1 sprig fresh thyme

2 bay leaves

Kosher salt and freshly ground pepper

⅓ cup (3 fl oz/80 ml) extra-virgin olive oil

12 *each* large shrimp, peeled and deveined, and jumbo scallops

½ lemon

2 zucchini, cut into ½-inch (12-mm) rounds

2 yellow bell peppers, cut into ¾-inch (2-cm) squares

1 yellow onion, cut into 1-inch (2-cm) squares

1 lb (500 g) cherry tomatoes, stemmed

Canola oil

MAKES 3–4 SERVINGS

White miso, which has a slightly sweet and mildly salty flavor, serves as the base for a flavorful marinade for these kabobs. With grilling, it becomes a pleasing glaze that coats the fish and green onions.

Marinated Tuna Skewers

- In a large glass bowl, whisk together the miso, sugar, vinegar, and ginger until the sugar dissolves. Add the tuna cubes and toss to coat the tuna well. Cover and refrigerate for 4–6 hours.

- Prepare a grill for direct-heat cooking over medium-high heat (page 134). Meanwhile, thread the tuna cubes and green onions, alternating, onto 6 metal skewers, dividing evenly. The green part of the green onion is thin and may require putting 2 or 3 pieces together as you skewer them in between the tuna.

- When the grill is hot, lightly oil the grill rack. Lay the skewers across the hottest part of the fire. Cook, turning frequently, until the tuna is nicely marked with grill marks and bright pink in the center for medium-rare, about 4 minutes total, or until cooked to your liking. Transfer to a platter and serve right away.

1 cup (8 oz/250 g) white miso

½ cup (4 oz/125 g) sugar

¾ cup (6 fl oz/180 ml) rice vinegar

1 tbsp minced fresh ginger

2 lb (1 kg) thick ahi tuna fillet, cut into 1- to 1¼-inch (2.5- to 3-cm) cubes

8 green onions, cut into 2-inch (5-cm) pieces

Canola oil

MAKES 6 SERVINGS

The mild acidity of yogurt is perfect for marinating this cold-water relative of salmon. Aromatic garam masala, redolent of cumin and coriander, imparts the flavors of Indian tandoori dishes.

Easy Tandoori Fish

⅓ cup (3 fl oz/80 ml) plain yogurt

4 tbsp (2 fl oz/60 ml) fresh lemon juice

1 tbsp garam masala

2 cloves garlic, minced

1 tbsp minced fresh ginger

Kosher salt and freshly ground black pepper

¼ tsp cayenne pepper

4 skin-on Arctic char fillets, 6 oz (185 g) each

1 cucumber, peeled and thinly sliced

½ red onion, thinly sliced

2 cups (14 oz/440 g) seeded and diced tomato

3 tbsp olive oil

2 tbsp minced fresh cilantro

MAKES 6 SERVINGS

● In a large glass bowl, stir together the yogurt, 2 tablespoons of the lemon juice, the garam masala, garlic, ginger, ½ teaspoon salt, a pinch of black pepper, and the cayenne. Add the fish fillets, coating them with the marinade. Cover and refrigerate for 2 hours.

● While the fish marinates, in a bowl, toss together the cucumber, onion, tomato, the remaining 2 tablespoons lemon juice, ½ teaspoon salt, a pinch of pepper, 1 tablespoon of the olive oil, and 1 tablespoon of the cilantro. Cover and refrigerate until serving time.

● Position the oven rack in the uppermost position and preheat the broiler. Line the bottom of a broiler pan with aluminum foil and place the rack on top. Remove the fish from the marinade and brush away the excess marinade. Drizzle the fillets with the remaining 2 tablespoons olive oil, and season lightly with salt and pepper. Arrange the fillets on the prepared pan so that they aren't touching. Broil until the fish is opaque throughout, about 4 minutes.

● Remove the fish from the oven, cover with foil, and let rest for 2 minutes. Serve right away with the cucumber salad alongside. Garnish with the remaining 1 tablespoon cilantro.

Broiling is an easy way to cook thick fish steaks. The popular combination of honey and mustard goes well with the rich flavor of salmon and caramelizes under the broiler to form a flavorful glaze.

Honey-Mustard Salmon

4 salmon steaks, each about 7 oz (220 g) and ¾ inch (2 cm) thick

Kosher salt and freshly ground pepper

1 tbsp fresh lemon juice

2 tbsp Dijon mustard

2 tbsp honey

1 tbsp olive oil

MAKES 4 SERVINGS

● About 30 minutes before cooking, remove the fish from the refrigerator. In a small dish, combine ½ teaspoon salt and ¼ teaspoon pepper and sprinkle it evenly over both sides of the salmon steaks. Set aside.

● In a small nonreactive bowl, whisk together the lemon juice, mustard, and honey until smooth.

● Choose a large, heavy frying pan with a heatproof handle, preferably cast iron, that will hold the steaks comfortably and withstand the high heat of the broiler (do not use nonstick). Position the oven rack so the top of the steaks will be 2–3 inches (5–7.5 cm) from the heat source. Place the pan in the oven and preheat the broiler for 10–15 minutes.

● When hot, use pot holders to remove the frying pan from the oven and place on the stove top over medium-high heat. Add the olive oil, swirling the pan to coat it lightly. Lay the salmon steaks in the pan and cook until the first sides are lightly browned, about 1 minute. Using a sturdy offset spatula, turn over the steaks and remove the pan from the heat.

● Working quickly, brush the honey-mustard glaze in a thick layer all over the top of the steaks. Put the pan under the broiler and cook until the glaze is browned and a skewer easily enters the center of the fish, about 4 minutes. Transfer the steaks to warmed plates and serve right away.

Mildly flavored mahimahi is a good vehicle for bold flavors, as this miso-and-mirin coated version shows. You can choose to add a thick or thin layer of the miso mixture to the fish—the choice is yours.

Miso-Glazed Mahimahi

- In a shallow bowl, combine the miso and mirin and stir until smooth. Add the fish steaks to the bowl and spread the paste all over the fish. Cover and refrigerate for at least 1 hour or up to overnight.

- About 30 minutes before cooking, remove the fish from the refrigerator. Choose a large, heavy frying pan with a heatproof handle, preferably cast iron, that will hold the steaks comfortably and withstand the high heat of the broiler (do not use nonstick). Position the oven rack so the top of the steaks will be 2–3 inches (5–7.5 cm) from the heat source. Place the pan in the oven and preheat the broiler for 10–15 minutes.

- When hot, use pot holders to remove the frying pan from the oven and place on the stove top over medium-high heat. Add the oil, swirling the pan to coat it lightly. Lay the steaks in the pan and cook until the first sides are lightly browned, about 2 minutes. Using a sturdy offset spatula, turn over the steaks and remove the pan from the heat.

- Working quickly, brush any remaining miso mixture in the bowl over the top of the steaks. Put the pan under the broiler and cook until the glaze is well browned and a skewer easily enters the center of the fish, 3–4 minutes. Transfer the steaks to warmed plates and serve right away.

3 tbsp white miso

3 tbsp mirin

4 mahimahi steaks, each about 6 oz (185 g) and ¾ inch (2 cm) thick

1 tbsp canola oil

MAKES 4 SERVINGS

Maple syrup and soy sauce come from different culinary traditions, but they combine beautifully in this rich glaze. Stronger flavors enhance swordfish, which is a firm, slightly oily, full-flavored fish.

Swordfish with Maple and Soy

4 swordfish steaks, each about 6 oz (185 g) and ¾ inch (2 cm) thick

Freshly ground pepper

3 tbsp pure maple syrup

3 tbsp low-sodium soy sauce

1 tbsp canola oil

MAKES 4 SERVINGS

● About 30 minutes before cooking, remove the fish from the refrigerator. Choose a large, heavy frying pan with a heatproof handle, preferably cast iron, that will hold the steaks comfortably and withstand the high heat of the broiler (do not use nonstick). Position the oven rack so the top of the steaks will be 2–3 inches (5–7.5 cm) from the heat source. Place the pan in the oven and preheat the broiler for 10–15 minutes.

● Season the swordfish steaks on both sides with ¼ teaspoon pepper and arrange on a plate. In a small saucepan over medium heat, combine the maple syrup and soy sauce. Bring to a boil and cook until reduced by half, about 2 minutes. Let cool, then brush about 1 tablespoon of the mixture on both sides of the steaks.

● Use pot holders to remove the hot frying pan from the oven and place on the stove top over medium-high heat. Add the oil, swirling the pan to coat it lightly. Lay the steaks in the pan and cook until the first sides are lightly browned, about 2 minutes. Using a sturdy offset spatula, turn over the steaks and remove the pan from the heat.

● Working quickly, brush the steaks with the remaining soy mixture. Put the pan under the broiler and cook until the glaze is thoroughly browned and a skewer easily enters the center of the fish, 3–4 minutes. Transfer the steaks to warmed plates and serve right away.

A generous coating of spices gives complex flavor and a touch of texture to mild halibut. The "warm" spices used here recall Indian-style curry powder, and toasting them enhances their exotic flavors.

Spice-Crusted Halibut

- In a small frying pan over low heat, combine the cardamom pods, cloves, cumin, coriander, fennel seeds, and peppercorns. Toast until fragrant, about 3 minutes, then immediately transfer to a plate to cool. Break open the cardamom pods and add the seeds to an electric spice grinder along with the rest of the spices; discard the cardamom hulls. Grind the spices to a coarse powder. Transfer to a small bowl and stir in the cinnamon.

- Prepare a grill for direct-heat cooking over medium-high heat (page 134). In a small saucepan over low heat, melt the butter with a large pinch of the spice mixture. Remove from the heat and keep warm. Lightly season the halibut steaks on one side with ¾ teaspoon salt, then sprinkle with a good ¼ teaspoon of the spice mixture and press gently to help it adhere. Repeat to coat the second sides, dividing the remaining spice mixture among them.

- When the grill is hot, lightly oil the grill rack. Lay the steaks on the hottest part of the grill. Cook until the steaks are opaque white halfway up the edges and show medium-brown grill marks, about 4 minutes. Use an offset spatula to turn the steaks and cook on the second side until a skewer easily enters the center, 2–3 minutes longer.

- Transfer the grilled steaks to a warmed platter, drizzle each steak with a little of the spiced butter, and serve right away.

12 cardamom pods

6 whole cloves

¾ tsp cumin seeds

¾ tsp coriander seeds

½ tsp fennel seeds

Scant ½ tsp peppercorns

¼ tsp ground cinnamon

3 tbsp unsalted butter

6 boneless halibut steaks, about 6 oz (185 g) each

Kosher salt

Canola oil

MAKES 6 SERVINGS

Salmon fillets, soaked in a spice-scented brine, are briefly smoked on a grill for a memorable main dish. A cucumber salad studded with capers and fragrant dill makes a refreshing accompaniment.

Brined Salmon with Cucumber Salad

- In a small saucepan, combine 1 cup (8 fl oz/250 ml) water, the cloves, and peppercorns. Bring to a boil. Remove from heat and let the mixture cool to room temperature. In a large glass bowl, stir together the spice-infused water, 7 cups (56 fl oz/ 1.75 l) cool water, the brown sugar, ¾ cup salt, and 2 tablespoons of the vinegar until the salt is dissolved to make a brine. Place the fish in the brine, skin side down, cover, and refrigerate for 3 hours.

- Remove the fish from the brine and rinse well. Pat dry and let air dry for 1 hour. Meanwhile, soak the wood chips in water to cover for about 1 hour.

- In a large glass bowl, whisk together the remaining ¼ cup vinegar, the granulated sugar, vegetable oil, and ½ teaspoon salt. Add the cucumbers, red onion, capers, and dill and toss to coat. Refrigerate until ready to serve.

- Prepare a grill for indirect-heat cooking over medium-high heat (page 135). If using charcoal, add the drained wood chips directly on top of the coals. If using gas, place the wood chips in a smoker box (page 135). Lay the salmon, skin side down, on the cooler side of the grill and cover. Cook until the fish is just barely cooked through, about 10 minutes.

- Transfer the salmon to a warmed platter and serve right away with the cucumber salad on the side.

10 *each* whole cloves and peppercorns

1 cup (7 oz/220 g) firmly packed light brown sugar

Kosher salt

6 tbsp (3 fl oz/90 ml) cider vinegar

6 thick skin-on salmon fillets, each about 6 oz (185 g)

1 handful hardwood chips

2 tbsp granulated sugar

¼ cup (2 fl oz/60 ml) vegetable oil

2 cucumbers, peeled and thinly sliced

½ cup (2 oz/60 g) thinly sliced red onion

2 tbsp capers

1 tbsp minced fresh dill

MAKES 6 SERVINGS

Here, simply grilled swordfish is accompanied by a mixture of sweet peppers, onions, and tomatoes. Slices of grilled rustic bread, brushed with garlicky olive oil, round out the dish.

Swordfish with Sweet Peppers

½ cup (4 fl oz/125 ml) extra-virgin olive oil

6 cloves garlic, sliced

2 large yellow onions, cut into ¼-inch (6-mm) slices

1 yellow bell pepper, seeded and chopped

2 red bell peppers, seeded and chopped

1½ tsp hot paprika

2 large tomatoes, seeded and chopped

Kosher salt and freshly ground pepper

4 swordfish steaks, each about 6 oz (185 g)

Canola oil

1 loaf ciabatta, halved crosswise

MAKES 4 SERVINGS

● In a small saucepan over low heat, combine 5 tablespoons of the oil and half of the garlic. Cook until the garlic is soft and fragrant, about 5 minutes. Remove from the heat, let cool, and then thoroughly mash the garlic against the side of the pan with a fork to make a paste. Set aside.

● In large heavy frying pan, warm 2 tablespoons of the remaining olive oil over medium heat. Add the onions, peppers, and remaining 3 garlic cloves and sauté until vegetables begin to soften, about 6 minutes. Add the paprika and cook for 1 minute. Add the tomatoes and sauté until soft, about 3 minutes. Season lightly with salt and pepper, remove from the heat, and set aside.

● Prepare a grill for direct-heat cooking over medium heat (page 134). Brush the swordfish with the remaining 1 tablespoon olive oil and season with salt and pepper.

● When the grill is hot, lightly oil the grill rack. Grill the fish directly over the heat, turning once, until just cooked through, about 4 minutes on each side.

● Meanwhile, brush the cut sides of the ciabatta with the garlic oil and season lightly with salt. Place the bread on the grill, cut side down, and cook until golden, about 4 minutes. Turn and continue to cook until golden, 2 minutes more. Remove from grill and cut into 2-inch (5-cm) slices.

● Arrange the swordfish on warm serving plates, spoon some of the pepper mixture over the tops, and serve right away with the grilled bread.

Chipotle chiles packed in adobo sauce lend a sweet and vinegary edge to a simple Mexican-inspired glaze. The spicy, smoky flavors are a perfect match for meaty broiled tuna steaks.

Tuna with Chipotle Glaze

4 ahi or albacore tuna steaks, each about 6 oz (185 g)

Kosher salt

3 tbsp fresh lime juice

1½ tbsp light brown sugar

½–1 canned chipotle chile in adobo sauce

1 tbsp canola oil

MAKES 4 SERVINGS

- About 30 minutes before cooking, remove the fish from the refrigerator.

- Choose a large, heavy frying pan with a heatproof handle, preferably cast iron, that will hold the steaks comfortably and withstand the high heat of the broiler (do not use nonstick). Position the oven rack so the top of the steaks will be 2–3 inches (5–7.5 cm) from the heat source. Place the pan in the oven and preheat the broiler.

- Season the tuna steaks on both sides with ½ teaspoon salt. In a small bowl, combine the lime juice and brown sugar. Using a spoon, push the chile though a fine-mesh sieve over the bowl; discard the solids in the sieve. Mix well and adjust the seasonings. Rub two-thirds of the chile mixture into the steaks on both sides.

- When hot, use pot holders to remove the frying pan from the oven and place on the stove top over medium-high heat. Add the oil, swirling the pan to coat it lightly. Lay the tuna steaks in the pan and cook until the first sides are lightly browned, about 2 minutes. Using a sturdy offset spatula, turn over the steaks and remove the pan from the heat.

- Working quickly, brush the steaks with the remaining chipotle mixture. Put the pan under the broiler and cook until the glaze darkens, but the center of the fish is still very pink, about 3 minutes for medium-rare, or until cooked to your liking. Transfer the steaks to warmed plates and serve right away.

This recipe utilizes the grill to its best: the delicate fish is cooked over the cooler part, while tortillas are warmed over the hot part. Add a lime-flavored slaw and you have a perfect summer supper.

Fish Tacos with Tangy Slaw

- In a bowl, stir together the mayonnaise and half of the lime juice. Add the cabbage, green onions, chile, and cilantro and mix well. Season to taste with salt and pepper, cover, and refrigerate the slaw until serving time.

- In a small bowl, mix together the cumin, oregano, and ½ teaspoon salt. Sprinkle the spice mixture evenly over both sides of the fish, then drizzle with the olive oil and remaining lime juice.

- Prepare a grill for indirect-heat cooking over medium-high heat (page 135). When the grill is hot, lightly oil the grill rack. Lay the fish fillets on the cooler part of the grill, cover, and cook, turning once, until the center of the fish looks opaque when pierced with the tip of a sharp knife, about 6 minutes total. During the last minute of grilling, place the tortillas on the grill, directly over the heat, and cook, turning once, until heated through and flexible.

- Transfer the tortillas and fish to a platter. To assemble, break up the fish into small pieces. Add a few pieces of fish and a large spoonful of slaw to each tortilla and fold in half. Serve right away.

⅓ cup (3 fl oz/80 ml) mayonnaise

Juice of 2 limes

½ head green cabbage, (about 12 oz/375 g), shredded

2 green onions, chopped

1 jalapeño chile, seeded and minced

2 tbsp chopped fresh cilantro

Kosher salt and freshly ground pepper

¼ tsp ground cumin

¼ tsp dried oregano

1 lb (500 g) snapper fillets

1 tbsp olive oil

Canola oil

12 corn tortillas

MAKES 4 SERVINGS

This recipe cleverly utilizes fresh herbs in two guises to infuse mild fish fillets with verdant flavor. It's a formula that can be used with other types of meaty fish, such as tuna, salmon, or swordfish.

Halibut with Fresh Herbs

2 bunches fresh
tarragon or thyme

Kosher salt and freshly
ground pepper

4 thick halibut fillets,
each about 6 oz (185 g)

Olive oil or
vegetable oil

MAKES 4 SERVINGS

- Chop about 1 tablespoon of the tarragon and set aside. Soak the remaining tarragon sprigs in cold water to cover for 15 minutes.

- Meanwhile, in a small bowl, mix together the chopped tarragon, 2 teaspoons salt, and 1 teaspoon pepper. Coat the halibut fillets with oil, then sprinkle the tarragon-salt mixture evenly on both sides of the fish.

- Prepare a grill for direct-heat cooking over medium-high heat (page 134). When the grill is hot, drain the tarragon sprigs and place them directly on the coals or grill burner. Lightly oil the grill rack. Lay the fish on the hottest part of the grill and cook, turning once, until opaque in the center and nicely marked with medium-brown grill marks, 3–4 minutes per side. Transfer to warmed plates and serve right away.

Cooking fish and shellfish quickly in hot oil—a little or a lot—is
a popular technique for the delicious crunch, golden finish, and
browned flavor it delivers. Sautéing and panfrying are arguably
the most versatile cooking methods and are perfect for most types

Sautéed & Fried

of seafood, from thin fillets to thick steaks to all kinds of shellfish.
Deep-frying and stir-frying are also delicious methods to employ
to get a fish dinner on the table any day of the week. The recipes that
follow will provide plenty of inspiration for every occasion, whether
it's a midweek supper or a weekend dinner with friends.

Fish for Sautéing & Frying

Many types of fish are suitable for sautéing and frying. Firm-fleshed white fish is a versatile option; try cod, halibut, catfish, striped bass, or trout. Thin fillets, such as flounder, sole, or skate, shine when sautéed or panfried and their clean flavor comes through. Most shellfish types can be sautéed or fried; mollusks should be shucked first.

Preparing to Cook

Keep fish and shellfish cold until just before cooking. Remove any errant bones (page 124) and rinse the fish well. Pat very dry with paper towels to keep the fish from steaming and encourage browning. Unless you are stir-frying, don't crowd the pan, which can also hinder the browning process; cook the fish in batches if necessary.

Deep-frying Fish

For deep-frying, fish is immersed in a generous amount of hot oil to create a golden brown crust. Coat the fish first with a batter or seasoned flour to protect it from the oil's heat and lend flavor. Choose a simple partner, such as a mayonnaise sauce, a squeeze of lemon, or malt vinegar, and serve the fish as soon as possible after cooking.

Tips & Tricks

Panfrying Fish

For panfrying, fish is cooked in a frying pan with a moderate amount of oil over moderately high heat. Dredge panfried fish in a flavorful coating, such as finely chopped nuts, bread crumbs, or thinly sliced potato, which will turn crisp in the fat and add flavor to the finished dish. Wipe out the pan before making pan sauces to remove any burned bits of coating.

Sautéing Fish

For sautéing, thin pieces of fish are quickly cooked in a small amount of fat over high heat. Watch the oil in the pan as it heats; when it appears to shimmer, you know it is hot enough for cooking. Take advantage of the browned bits left in the pan by dissolving them in wine or stock. Called deglazing, this forms the base for a complementary pan sauce.

Stir-frying Fish

For stir-frying, small pieces of fish are rapidly cooked over very high heat, while constantly stirring and tossing. For best results, cut all your ingredients into similar-sized pieces so that they cook at the same rate. Be sure to have all your ingredients prepped and arranged near the stove before you begin cooking, as the process goes very quickly.

Few dishes are more irresistible than the duo of perfectly fried fish and potatoes. Deep-frying gives them a light, crisp texture and golden color difficult to achieve with any other cooking method.

Classic Fish & Chips

● Preheat the oven to 200°F (95°C). Clip a deep-frying thermometer to the side of a large, deep, heavy pot. Fill the pot no more than half full with the oil, place over high heat, and heat the oil until it reaches 300°F (150°C). Line 2 rimmed baking sheets with paper towels. Place a wire rack on 1 sheet.

● Drain the potatoes and pat very dry. In batches, cook the potatoes until blistered but not brown, about 5 minutes, then transfer to the paper towel–lined sheet to cool. Adjust the heat as needed to maintain the oil temperature.

● Increase the heat to high and heat the oil until it reaches 360°–375°F (182°–190°C). In batches, fry the cooled potatoes a second time until golden brown and crisp, 4–5 minutes. Keep warm in the oven.

● Reduce the heat so that the oil reads 350°F (180°C). Cut the fish into 12 equal pieces and season lightly. In a bowl, whisk together the ¾ cup flour with ¼ teaspoon salt. Slowly whisk in the beer just until all the flour is moistened. Dredge 3 or 4 fish pieces in flour, shake off the excess, and slide into the beer batter. Using tongs, lift the fish pieces one by one from the batter and lower into the hot oil. Fry until golden brown, about 3 minutes, turning the pieces over once. Transfer to the sheet with the wire rack and keep warm in the oven. Adjust the heat as needed to maintain the oil temperature. Continue to batter and fry the remaining fish pieces.

● Sprinkle the fish and potatoes with salt and transfer to warmed plates. Pass the lemon wedges, malt vinegar, or aioli at the table.

1–2 qt (1–2 l) peanut, corn, or canola oil

3 thin-skinned russet potatoes, about 1½ lb (750 g) total weight, cut into ³⁄₈-inch (1-cm) sticks and soaked in cold water to cover

1½–2 lb (750 g–1 kg) skinned firm white fish fillets such as cod, pollock, or halibut

Kosher salt and freshly ground pepper

¾ cup (4 oz/125 g) all-purpose flour, plus more for dredging

1 cup (8 fl oz/250 ml) brown or amber ale

Lemon wedges, malt vinegar, or Aioli (page 139) for serving

MAKES 6 SERVINGS

No one can resist fried shrimp, especially when paired with a favorite sauce for dipping. Nearly halving—or butterflying—the shrimp increases their surface area so they cook especially fast.

Fried Butterflied Shrimp

- Lay each shrimp on its side and, using a small, sharp knife, make a deep cut along the outer curve, stopping short of cutting the shrimp in half. Spread the halves apart and pick out the vein, if present. When all the shrimp have been butterflied, sprinkle with 2 teaspoons salt, let stand for 1 minute, then rinse well and pat dry.

- To a bowl, add 1 cup (8 fl oz/250 ml) water. Sift ½ cup (2½ oz/75 g) of the flour into the bowl with water and whisk to combine to make a batter. Place the remaining 1 cup (5 oz/155 g) flour in another bowl.

- Preheat the oven to 200°F (95°C). Clip a deep-frying thermometer to the side of a deep pot and pour in the oil to a depth of at least 1½ inches (4 cm) but no more than half full. Place over high heat and heat to 375°F (190°C). Line a rimmed baking sheet with paper towels and place a wire rack on top.

- Working with 1 small handful at a time, toss the shrimp in the flour, shake to remove the excess flour, and drop into the batter. Using a wire skimmer, lift the shrimp out of the batter, let the excess drip back into the bowl, and lower into the hot oil. Fry until crisp and light brown, turning occasionally, 1–2 minutes. Transfer to the wire rack and keep warm in the oven while you repeat to batter and fry the remaining shrimp. Serve right away with the lemon wedges or sauce.

1 lb (500 g) medium shrimp, peeled, tails intact

Kosher salt

1½ cups (7½ oz/230 g) all-purpose flour

Peanut, corn, or canola oil

Lemon wedges, Aioli (page 139), or Tartar Sauce (page 139) for serving

MAKES 2–3 SERVINGS

Cloaked with a light, crisp batter, this Italian-inspired recipe has something for everyone. Vary it by using more or less of each type of shellfish, and providing one or more dipping sauces.

Mixed Seafood Fry

1 cup (5 oz/155 g) all-purpose flour

Kosher salt and freshly ground pepper

1 cup (8 fl oz/250 ml) whole milk

2 large eggs, separated

1 tbsp olive oil

Canola oil

½ lb (250 g) cleaned squid bodies (page 131), cut into rings ¼ inch (6 mm) wide

12 large shrimp, peeled, tails intact, and deveined

1 lb (500 g) *each* oysters and small hard-shelled clams, shucked (pages 129 and 130)

2 tbsp minced fresh flat-leaf parsley

Lemon wedges

MAKES 6 SERVINGS

● In a bowl, combine the flour, ½ teaspoon salt, and ¼ teaspoon pepper. Stir in the milk, egg yolks, and olive oil until blended. In another bowl, beat the egg whites until soft peaks form. Carefully fold the beaten egg whites into the milk mixture just until blended to make a batter.

● Preheat the oven to 200°F (95°C). Clip a deep-frying thermometer to the side of a deep pot and pour in the oil to a depth of at least 1½ inches (4 cm) but no more than half full. Place over high heat and heat to 375°F (190°C). Line a rimmed baking sheet with paper towels and place a wire rack on top.

● Pat the seafood very dry. Working in batches, dip the squid, shrimp, clams, and oysters in the batter. Using a wire skimmer, lift the seafood out of the batter, let the excess drip back into the bowl, and lower into the hot oil. Fry until crisp and golden brown, turning once, about 1 minute for the squid, 1½ minutes for the clams and oysters, and 2 minutes for the shrimp. Transfer to the wire rack and keep warm in the oven while you repeat to batter and fry the remaining shellfish.

● Sprinkle with the parsley and serve right away accompanied by the lemon wedges for squeezing.

Finely chopped nuts make a crisp coating for sautéed fillets. Here the fish gets dressed up with a New Orleans–style sauce based on a brown butter-and-flour mixture that deepens the pecans' flavor.

Pecan-Crusted Catfish

3 tbsp unsalted butter

3 tbsp all-purpose flour

Kosher salt and freshly ground pepper

Scant ½ tsp hot paprika

6 skinned catfish fillets, about 2 lb (1 kg) total weight

1 cup (4 oz/125 g) pecan halves, finely chopped

4 tbsp peanut, corn, or canola oil

2 green onions, white parts minced and green parts thinly sliced

⅓ cup (3 fl oz/80 ml) dry sherry

1½ cups (12 fl oz/ 375 ml) Fish Fumet (page 138) or low-sodium chicken broth

MAKES 6 SERVINGS

● In a small saucepan over medium-low heat, melt the butter. Stir in the flour and cook, stirring frequently, until the mixture is a rich, even medium brown, about 10 minutes. Set aside.

● In a small bowl, mix together 1½ teaspoons salt, ¼ teaspoon pepper, and the paprika. Sprinkle about two-thirds of the mixture evenly over both sides of the fish. Pour the nuts on a plate. Place a large frying pan over low heat. Press the boned side of each fillet into the nuts, patching bare spots as needed.

● Add 2 tablespoons of the oil to the pan and swirl to coat. Raise the heat to medium. When the oil shimmers, add half of the fillets, coated side down. Cook until the nuts form a golden brown crust, about 4 minutes. Turn the fillets and cook until a skewer easily enters the thickest part of the fillets, 2–4 minutes longer. Transfer to warmed plates. Wipe out the pan and add the remaining 2 tablespoons oil. Cook the second batch of fillets in the same manner.

● Wipe out the pan, add the minced onion, and cook until fragrant, a few seconds. Add the sherry and cook until nearly evaporated, less than 1 minute. Add the fumet and the remaining seasoned salt (omit if using canned broth), and bring to a boil. Stir the browned flour mixture until smooth, then whisk into the pan. Cook, whisking, until smooth and lightly thickened. Taste and adjust the seasonings.

● Spoon the sauce on the plates around the fish. Garnish with the sliced onions and serve right away.

Japanese-style bread crumbs, called panko, lend these fillets an appealing crisp coating after panfrying. Paired with an easy soy-based dipping sauce, it evokes tempura without all the work.

Cod with Ginger-Soy Dipping Sauce

- In a small bowl, mix together ¾ teaspoon salt and a pinch of freshly ground pepper. Sprinkle evenly on both sides of the fillets. Place the flour, egg whites, and bread crumbs in separate shallow bowls near the stove.

- Divide the minced ginger among 6 dipping bowls. To each bowl, add 1 teaspoon each of the lemon juice and soy sauce and stir to combine.

- In a large frying pan over medium heat, heat the oil. Coat a piece of fish in the flour and shake off the excess. Slide it into the egg whites and turn to coat evenly, then transfer it to the bread crumbs. Scoop the crumbs over the top to coat the fish. Transfer the coated fillet to a plate and repeat to coat the remaining fish.

- In 2 batches, add the fish fillets to the pan and cook until golden brown on the first side, 2–3 minutes. Turn and brown the second side, 1–3 minutes longer. Add more oil to the pan if needed to prevent sticking.

- As the fillets are done, transfer them to warmed plates. Serve right away with the dipping sauce on the side.

Kosher salt and freshly ground pepper

2 lb (1 kg) skinned cod fillets, cut into 6 equal portions

½ cup (2½ oz/75 g) all-purpose flour

2 large egg whites, lightly beaten

1 cup (4 oz/125 g) *panko* bread crumbs

1 tbsp minced fresh ginger

2 tbsp fresh lemon juice

2 tbsp soy sauce

About 2 tbsp peanut oil

MAKES 6 SERVINGS

Here, salmon fillets are seared on the stove top until still pink in the center then are topped with a unique, Asian-inspired herb sauce. The complex flavors in the dish belie how easy it is to make.

Salmon with Asian Pesto

2 cloves garlic, chopped

1 jalapeño chile, chopped

3 green onions, chopped

3 tbsp *each* chopped fresh cilantro and basil

3 tbsp peanut oil

2 tbsp Asian fish sauce

Juice of ½ lime

1 tsp sugar

4 salmon fillets, about 6 oz (185 g) each

Salt and freshly ground pepper

MAKES 4 SERVINGS

● Add the garlic, chile, green onions, cilantro, basil, and 1 tablespoon water to a blender and process to make a paste.

● In a small frying pan over medium heat, warm 2 tablespoons of the oil. Add the herb paste and sauté until fragrant, 1–2 minutes. Stir in the fish sauce, 2 tablespoons water, the lime juice, and sugar. Cook, stirring, until the sugar is dissolved and the flavors are blended, about 2 minutes.

● Season the fillets lightly with salt and pepper.

● Heat a large frying pan over high heat until very hot and add the remaining 1 tablespoon oil. Add the salmon to the pan and cook until golden brown on the undersides, about 2 minutes. Turn the fillets and cook until the second sides are golden brown and the fish is still slightly rare in the center, about 2 minutes more.

● Transfer the fillets to warmed individual plates and drizzle with the pesto. Serve right away.

This version of crab cakes uses just enough bread crumbs and mayonnaise to bind the mixture, without distracting from the flavor of the crab. Serve the cakes with a vinaigrette-dressed salad.

Crab Cakes with Aioli

- In a bowl, stir together the crabmeat and bread crumbs. Add the mayonnaise, Worcestershire sauce, mustard, paprika, green onion, parsley, ½ teaspoon salt, and ¼ teaspoon pepper, to the bowl with the crabmeat. Mix gently with a fork until evenly moistened but some good-sized chunks of crab remain. Stir in the egg whites. Refrigerate until ready to cook.

- In a large frying pan over medium heat, heat 2 tablespoons canola oil. Pack some of the crab mixture into a ⅓ cup (3 fl oz/80 ml) dry measuring cup. Turn the cup over and tap the edge sharply on a plate to form a neat cake. Using an offset spatula, transfer the cake to the pan and repeat to form the remaining cakes, adding each to the pan as you go. Cook the cakes until browned on both sides and heated through, 3–5 minutes per side. Transfer each cake to a paper towel–lined plate. Add more oil to the pan if needed to prevent sticking.

- Arrange the crab cakes on individual plates and serve right away with the Aioli.

1 lb (500 g) fresh crabmeat

¼ cup (1 oz/30 g) fine dried bread crumbs

2 tbsp best-quality mayonnaise

1 tsp Worcestershire sauce

1 tsp Dijon mustard

½ tsp hot paprika

1 tbsp minced green onion

1 tbsp minced fresh flat-leaf parsley

Kosher salt and freshly ground pepper

2 large egg whites, lightly beaten

Canola oil

Aioli (page 139)

MAKES 4 SERVINGS

Sorrel, a refreshing, lemon-flavored herb, is a nice alternative to lemon juice or wine in this simple sauce to pour over quick-sautéed mild fish fillets. Sole is a good substitute if flounder is unavailable.

Flounder with Herb Butter

- In a small frying pan over low heat, melt the butter until the foam subsides. Add the sorrel slivers and a pinch of salt. Stir gently as the sorrel wilts, about 1 minute. Remove from the heat and cover to keep warm.

- In a small bowl, stir together 1 teaspoon salt and ¼ teaspoon pepper. Sprinkle evenly over both sides of the fillets.

- In a large frying pan over medium-high heat, heat 1 tablespoon of the olive oil. Coat half of the fillets with the flour and shake off the excess. Add the fillets to the pan and cook until the edges are opaque and the bottoms are golden brown, about 2 minutes. Turn the fillets and cook on the second side until a skewer easily enters the thickest part, 1–2 minutes longer. Transfer to warmed plates. Add the remaining 1 tablespoon olive oil to the pan and cook the second batch of fillets in the same manner. Spoon the sauce over the fish and serve right away.

6 tbsp (3 oz/90 g) unsalted butter

3 oz (60 g) sorrel leaves, cut into thin slivers

Kosher salt and freshly ground pepper

2 lb (1 kg) skinned flounder fillets

2 tbsp olive oil

½ cup (2½ oz/75 g) all-purpose flour

MAKES 6 SERVINGS

The sauce for this French-inspired recipe is made by browning butter until nut colored, and then adding tart capers to offset its richness. Skate can be hard to find, but sole or flounder are good substitutes.

Skate with Capers & Brown Butter

6 tbsp (3 oz/90 g) unsalted butter

2 tsp rinsed and drained capers

Kosher salt and freshly ground pepper

2 lb (1 kg) skinned skate fillets, cut into 6 equal portions

2 tbsp olive oil

½ cup (2½ oz/75 g) all-purpose flour

MAKES 6 SERVINGS

• In a small frying pan over low heat, melt the butter until it begins to turn golden brown, 3–4 minutes. Add the capers, remove from the heat, and cover to keep warm.

• In a small bowl, stir together 1 teaspoon salt and ¼ teaspoon pepper. Sprinkle evenly over both sides of the fillets.

• In a large frying pan over medium heat, heat 1 tablespoon of the olive oil. Coat half of the fillets with the flour and shake off the excess. Add the fillets to the pan and cook until the edges are opaque and the bottoms are golden brown, about 3 minutes. Turn the fillets and cook on the second side until a skewer easily enters the thickest part, about 2 minutes longer. Transfer to warmed plates. Add the remaining 1 tablespoon olive oil to the pan and cook the second batch of fillets in the same manner. Spoon the butter sauce over the fish and serve right away.

Delicately flavored with a firm, flaky texture, sole is a versatile fish. Here, it's quickly sautéed, then the drippings are combined with butter, lemon juice, and parsley for a quick but flavorful pan sauce.

Sole with Lemon & Parsley

Kosher salt

⅛ tsp hot paprika

2 lb (1 kg) skinned sole fillets

½ cup (2½ oz/75 g) all-purpose flour

About 2 tbsp olive oil

1 shallot, minced

2 tbsp minced fresh flat-leaf parsley

⅓ cup (3 fl oz/80 ml) Fish Fumet (page 138) or water

¼ cup (2 fl oz/60 ml) fresh lemon juice

3 tbsp unsalted butter, at room temperature

Freshly ground pepper, optional

MAKES 6 SERVINGS

● In a small bowl, mix together ¾ teaspoon salt and the paprika. Sprinkle evenly over both sides of the fillets. Pour the flour into a shallow bowl.

● Heat a large frying pan over medium-high heat. Meanwhile, coat half of the fillets with flour, then shake off the excess. Add 1 tablespoon of the olive oil to the pan. When the oil shimmers, add about half of the fillets to the pan in a single layer. Cook until the edges are opaque all around and the bottoms are golden brown, about 2 minutes. Using a wide spatula, turn the fillets and cook on the second side until a skewer easily enters the thickest part, about 1 minute longer. Transfer the fillets to warmed plates. While the first batch is cooking, coat the second batch of fillets with flour. Add the remaining 1 tablespoon oil to the pan and cook the second batch of fillets in the same manner.

● Add the shallot and parsley to the pan, adding a touch more oil if the pan seems dry. Cook for a few seconds, then stir in the fumet, scraping the bottom of the pan to loosen any browned bits. Add the lemon juice and boil until the liquid has almost completely evaporated, about 1 minute. Stir in the butter until it melts. Taste and adjust the seasonings. Spoon the sauce over the fish and serve right away.

Toasting and grinding fragrant spices is a small step that gives this pan-fried tilapia a big boost in flavor. Sweet corn, fresh tomatoes, and green onions are made into a relish for a fresh counterpoint.

Spiced Tilapia with Corn Relish

- In a small dry frying pan over medium heat, combine the coriander and cumin seeds. Toast, stirring constantly, until fragrant, 2–3 minutes. Let cool and transfer to an electric spice mill and grind to a fine powder. Transfer to a small bowl and stir in the cinnamon, 1 teaspoon salt, and ¼ teaspoon pepper. Reserve ½ teaspoon of the spice blend for the relish.

- In a frying pan over medium-high heat, heat the 1 teaspoon oil. Add the corn and sauté until lightly browned, about 3 minutes. Add the garlic, ¼ teaspoon salt, ¼ teaspoon pepper, and the reserved spice blend, and sauté until fragrant, about 1 minute. Pour into a large bowl and let cool slightly. Add the tomatoes, green onions, 1 tablespoon of the olive oil, the honey, and vinegar and mix well. Season to taste and set aside.

- Brush both sides of the fillets lightly with 1 tablespoon of the oil. Sprinkle the spice mixture over both sides and press down lightly to adhere.

- In a large frying over medium heat, heat the remaining 1 tablespoon oil. When the oil shimmers, add the fillets and cook, turning once, until golden brown and a skewer easily enters the fish, 2–3 minutes per side.

- Transfer the fillets to warmed plates, spoon some of the corn relish over the fish, and serve right away.

1 tbsp coriander seeds

1 tsp cumin seeds

½ tsp ground cinnamon

Kosher salt and freshly ground pepper

3 tbsp plus 1 tsp extra-virgin olive oil

1½ cups (9 oz/280 g) fresh corn kernels

2 cloves garlic, minced

1 cup (6 oz/185 g) peeled, seeded, and diced tomatoes

¼ cup (¾ oz/25 g) finely chopped green onions

1 tbsp honey

1 tbsp white wine vinegar

4 tilapia fillets, each about 6 oz (185 g)

MAKES 4 SERVINGS

Olivada, the Italian version of French tapenade, is an olive spread with garlic, capers, lemon zest, and herbs. It's a powerhouse of flavor and the perfect topping for mild, firm-fleshed halibut.

Halibut with Olive-Garlic Paste

1 cup (5 oz/155 g) pitted kalamata olives

1 clove garlic, minced

1½ tbsp capers, preferably salt-packed, rinsed

1 tsp grated lemon zest

1 tbsp fresh lemon juice

2 tbsp chopped fresh flat-leaf parsley

1 tsp chopped fresh thyme

Kosher salt and freshly ground pepper

4 tbsp (2 fl oz/60 ml) extra-virgin olive oil

6 halibut fillets, each about 6 oz (185 g)

MAKES 6 SERVINGS

● In a food processor, combine the olives, garlic, capers, lemon zest, lemon juice, parsley, thyme, ¼ teaspoon pepper, and 2 tablespoons of the olive oil. Pulse several times until the ingredients are combined, but still chunky. Set aside.

● In a small bowl, mix together 1 teaspoon salt and ¼ teaspoon pepper. Sprinkle evenly over both sides of the fillets.

● In a large frying pan over medium-high heat, heat 1 tablespoon of the oil. Add half of the fillets and cook until the edges are opaque and the bottoms are golden brown, about 3 minutes. Turn the fillets and cook on the second side until a skewer easily enters the thickest part, 2–3 minutes more. Transfer the fillets to warmed plates. Add the remaining 1 tablespoon oil to the pan and cook the second batch of fillets in the same manner.

● Top each fillet with a generous dollop of the olive mixture and serve right away.

Here is a great way to use leftover salmon, especially poached salmon. Crown the hash with a poached egg and spoon hollandaise sauce (page 72) over the top for a sophisticated presentation.

Salmon Hash

- Peel the potatoes and cut them into ½-inch (12-mm) dice.

- In a large frying pan over medium-high heat, heat the oil. Add the onion and sauté until softened, about 5 minutes. Add the potatoes, reduce the heat to medium, cover, and cook, stirring and scraping the bottom of the pan often, until they are almost tender but still hold their shape, about 15 minutes. Add 1 tablespoon water if the pan seems too dry.

- Stir in the cream, reduce the heat to medium, and simmer gently, stirring from time to time, until the potatoes are soft, 8–10 minutes. During the last 5 minutes of cooking, stir in the dill and salmon and heat through. Taste and adjust the seasoning.

- Divide the hash among warmed serving plates and serve right away.

3 Yukon gold potatoes, about 1 lb (500 g) total weight

2 tbsp olive oil

1 yellow onion, chopped

½ cup (4 fl oz/125 ml) heavy cream

1 tsp chopped fresh dill

1 lb (500 g) cooked salmon, broken into bite-sized pieces

Kosher salt and freshly ground pepper

MAKES 6 SERVINGS

Here, slivered almonds are toasted to bring out their nutty flavor, then combined with shallots, fresh lemon juice, and butter to make a rich but tangy pan sauce for quickly cooked trout fillets.

Trout with Almonds

- In a small, dry frying pan over medium-low heat, toast the almonds, stirring constantly, until golden brown and fragrant, about 5 minutes. Set aside.

- In a small bowl, mix together 1 teaspoon salt and ¼ teaspoon pepper. Sprinkle evenly over the flesh side of the fillets.

- In a large frying pan over medium-high heat, heat 1 tablespoon of the olive oil. Coat half of the fillets with the flour, then shake off the excess. When the oil shimmers, add half of the fillets to the pan and cook until the edges are opaque and the bottoms are golden brown, about 2 minutes. Turn the fillets and cook on the second side until a skewer easily enters the thickest part, about 2 minutes longer. Transfer the fillets to warmed plates. While the first batch is cooking, coat the second batch of fillets with flour. Add the remaining 1 tablespoon oil to the pan and cook the second batch of fillets in the same manner.

- Add the shallots to the pan and cook until fragrant, 1–2 minutes. Add the lemon juice, butter, and toasted almonds, stirring constantly, until the butter melts. Taste and adjust the seasonings. Spoon the sauce over the fish and serve right away.

⅓ cup (1½ oz/45 g) slivered blanched almonds

Kosher salt and freshly ground pepper

6 skin-on trout fillets, about 2 lb (1 kg) total weight

2 tbsp olive oil

½ cup (2½ oz/75 g) all-purpose flour

2 tbsp minced shallots

2 tbsp fresh lemon juice

3 tbsp unsalted butter

MAKES 6 SERVINGS

The exotic flavor of five-spice powder goes well with the nutty flavor of the bread crumb crust that coats fresh trout fillets. It's an unusual, but delicious fusion of east-west flavors for a quick dinner.

Trout with Bread Crumbs

½ tsp Chinese five-spice powder

Kosher salt

6 skin-on trout fillets, about 2 lb (1 kg) total weight

⅓ cup (1½ oz/ 45 g) plain dried bread crumbs

Peanut or canola oil

3 tbsp unsalted butter

MAKES 6 SERVINGS

● In a small bowl, mix together the five-spice powder and ½ teaspoon salt and sprinkle generously on the flesh side of the fillets, saving a pinch for the sauce.

● Heat a large frying pan over low heat. Meanwhile, spread the bread crumbs on a plate and press the flesh side of the fillets into the crumbs to coat.

● Add 1 tablespoon oil to the pan and raise the heat to medium. When the oil shimmers, add half of the fillets to the pan, coated side down. Cook until the crumbs form a golden brown crust, 2–3 minutes. Turn the fillets and cook on the second side, 1–3 minutes longer. Add more oil to the pan as needed to prevent sticking. Transfer the fillets to warmed plates. Add 1 tablespoon oil to the pan and cook the second batch of fillets in the same manner.

● Wipe out any excess oil from the pan and add the butter and the reserved spice mixture. Cook, stirring, until the butter melts and begins to brown. Taste and adjust the seasonings. Spoon the sauce over the fish and serve right away.

Pan-searing scallops develops a pleasing browned exterior, which contrasts with the sweet meat of the shellfish. Here, they're paired with an easy but elegant butter sauce made with fresh orange juice.

Scallops with Orange Sauce

¼ cup (2 fl oz/60 ml) fresh orange juice

2 tbsp white wine vinegar

½ shallot, minced

½ cup (4 oz/125 g) unsalted butter, cut into 16 pieces, chilled

Kosher salt and freshly ground white pepper

1 lb (500 g) large scallops

1 tbsp olive oil or canola oil

Grated zest of 1 orange, optional

MAKES 4–6 SERVINGS

- In a small nonreactive saucepan over medium-high heat, combine the orange juice, vinegar, and shallot and bring to a boil. Reduce the heat to low and simmer until the mixture has reduced in volume to become a thick paste, 5–7 minutes. Let cool slightly.

- Set the pan over the lowest possible heat, add 2 pieces of the butter, and stir until melted. Continue adding butter gradually, stirring constantly as it melts, until all the butter is incorporated into the sauce. Taste and adjust the seasonings. Keep the sauce in a warm place, but not over direct heat.

- Place a large frying pan over medium-high heat until thoroughly heated. Meanwhile, season the scallops on both sides with ¼ teaspoon salt and ⅛ teaspoon white pepper. Add the oil to the hot pan and swirl to coat. When the oil shimmers, add the scallops in a single layer and cook until nicely browned on the first side, about 1½ minutes. Turn the scallops and cook until slightly springy when pressed, about 2 minutes.

- Transfer the scallops to warmed plates. Spoon the sauce around the scallops, garnish with the orange zest, if using, and serve right away.

Spanish chorizo, a smoky, paprika-laced sausage, adds a slightly spicy element to this international version of shrimp and grits. Parmesan-infused polenta is a sophisticated, but simple, base.

Shrimp with Sausage & Polenta

- Make the polenta according to the recipe. While the polenta is cooking, heat the oil in a large frying pan over medium heat. Add the shrimp and sauté until just opaque, 1–2 minutes. Transfer the shrimp to a warmed plate.

- Add the onion to the pan and sauté until softened, about 3 minutes. Cut the chorizo into ½-inch (12-mm) chunks, add to the pan, and sauté until browned. Add the garlic and sauté until fragrant, about 1 minute. Sprinkle the flour over the sausage and sauté for 2 minutes. Whisk in the wine and tomatoes and cook until the liquid is almost evaporated, 2–3 minutes. Add the broth and cook until slightly thickened, about 3 minutes. Add the cream and half of the green onions and simmer to blend the flavors, about 3 minutes. Return the shrimp to the pan and cook until heated through, about 1 minute. Season to taste with salt and pepper.

- Pour the polenta into warmed serving bowls. Spoon the shrimp and chorizo mixture over the top, garnish with the remaining green onions, and serve right away.

Creamy Polenta (page 139)

2 tbsp extra-virgin olive oil

2 lb (1 kg), large shrimp, peeled and deveined

1 onion, minced

1 lb (500 g) Spanish-style chorizo

2 cloves garlic, minced

1 tbsp all-purpose flour

½ cup (4 fl oz/125 ml) dry white wine

1 cup (6 oz/185 g) canned diced tomatoes

1 cup (8 fl oz/250 ml) low-sodium chicken broth

¼ cup (2 fl oz/60 ml) heavy cream

2 green onions, sliced

Kosher salt and freshly ground pepper

MAKES 6 SERVINGS

Salting the shrimp and letting it stand for about 15 minutes before cooking imparts great flavor. The quick sauté, enhanced with hearty greens, means dinner is on the table in no time.

Garlicky Shrimp & Swiss Chard

1 lb (500 g) large shrimp, peeled and deveined

Kosher salt

⅓ cup (3 fl oz/80 ml) extra-virgin olive oil

2 bunches Swiss chard, thick ribs removed, chopped

2 tbsp chopped garlic

½ tsp red pepper flakes

Grated zest and juice of 1 orange

1 bay leaf

2 tbsp minced fresh flat-leaf parsley

MAKES 4 SERVINGS

● Place the shrimp in a bowl, add 1 teaspoon salt, and toss thoroughly. Refrigerate for 15 minutes.

● In a frying pan over high heat, heat half of the oil. Add the chard, 1 tablespoon of the garlic, ¼ teaspoon of the red pepper flakes, and ¼ teaspoon salt. Sauté until the chard is wilted and tender, about 3 minutes. Transfer to a warmed platter and sprinkle with the orange zest. Cover to keep warm.

● Add the remaining oil to the pan. When the oil shimmers, add the shrimp, the remaining 1 tablespoon garlic, the remaining ¼ teaspoon red pepper flakes, and the bay leaf and sauté until the shrimp starts to turn opaque, about 1 minute. Add the orange juice and continute to sauté, stirring to dislodge the browned bits on the bottom of the pan, until the shrimp is opaque throughout, about 1 minute more.

● Arrange the shrimp on top of the chard and drizzle the orange sauce over the top. Garnish with the parsley and serve right away.

The term "scampi" is often used to describe a dish of large shrimp cooked with lots of garlic. This version adds fresh parsley, lemon zest, and lemon juice, to make a complementary pan sauce.

Shrimp Scampi

- In a bowl, sprinkle the shrimp with 1 tablespoon salt and toss to coat evenly. Let stand for no more than 1 minute, then rinse well and drain. Pat the shrimp dry.

- Place a large frying pan over medium heat and add the oil. When the oil shimmers, add the shrimp and cook until bright orange on one side, about 2 minutes. Turn with tongs and continue cooking until the shrimp are opaque throughout, 1–3 minutes longer. Transfer to a warmed platter.

- In a small bowl, mix together the garlic, parsley, and lemon zest. Add two-thirds of the mixture and a pinch of pepper to the pan. Sauté until fragrant but not browned, about 30 seconds. Add the lemon juice and ¼ cup (2 fl oz/60 ml) water and bring to a boil, scraping up the browned bits from the bottom of the pan. Cook until the liquid is nearly evaporated, remove from the heat, and add the butter. Stir quickly and constantly as the butter melts. Taste and adjust the seasonings.

- Return the shrimp to the pan, stir to coat with the sauce, and transfer to warmed plates. Sprinkle the remaining parsley-garlic mixture on top and serve right away.

1½ lb (750 g) large shrimp, peeled, with tail sections intact, and deveined

Kosher salt and freshly ground pepper

1 tbsp olive oil

2 cloves garlic, thinly sliced

4–6 sprigs fresh flat-leaf parsley, minced

Grated zest of 1 large lemon

2 tbsp fresh lemon juice

2–3 tbsp cold unsalted butter, cut into 6 pieces

MAKES 4 SERVINGS

This dish features grassy asparagus, citrusy lemongrass, and bright, fresh mint for a quintessential springtime dish. Shrimp are perfect candidates for a stir-fry as they cook quickly.

Shrimp & Asparagus Stir-Fry

- In a large bowl, toss together the shrimp, garlic, ginger, 1 tablespoon of the canola oil, and ¼ teaspoon salt. Let stand for 30 minutes. Cut the asparagus into 1-inch (2.5-cm) sections.

- In a small bowl, combine the soy sauce, vinegar, wine, honey, cornstarch, and sesame oil. Set aside.

- Heat a wok or large frying pan over high heat and add 1 tablespoon of the canola oil. When the oil begins to smoke, add the shrimp and stir-fry until almost cooked through, about 2 minutes. Transfer the shrimp to a bowl and keep warm.

- Add the remaining 1 tablespoon oil to the wok along with the minced shallots and lemongrass and stir-fry until fragrant, about 1 minute. Add the asparagus and stir-fry until tender-crisp, about 2 minutes. Add the soy mixture to the wok along with the shrimp and stir-fry until the shrimp are opaque throughout, about 2 minutes.

- Sprinkle the mint over the stir-fry and serve right away.

1 lb (500 g) large shrimp, peeled and deveined

1 bunch asparagus

2 cloves garlic, minced

1½ tbsp minced fresh ginger

3 tbsp canola oil

Kosher salt

⅓ cup (3 fl oz/80 ml) soy sauce

¼ cup (2 fl oz/60 ml) *each* rice vinegar and dry white wine

2 tbsp honey

2 tsp *each* cornstarch and Asian sesame oil

⅓ cup (2 oz/60 g) minced shallots

3 tbsp thinly sliced lemongrass bulb

2 tbsp chopped fresh mint

MAKES 4 SERVINGS

Chinese black beans have a sharp, pungent, but slightly sweet flavor that pairs well with the rich sweetness of Dungeness crab. Be sure to provide plenty of napkins, as this dish is deliciously messy.

Crab with Black Bean Sauce

2 Dungeness crabs, cooked and cleaned (page 132)

3 tbsp fermented black beans

1 tsp sugar

2 cloves garlic, minced

2 tsp minced fresh ginger

1 tsp chile-garlic sauce

2 tsp soy sauce

2 tbsp rice vinegar

2 tbsp canola oil

MAKES 6 SERVINGS

● Rinse and pat dry the crab thoroughly. Remove the top shell and discard. Remove the legs and claws and set aside. With a cleaver, cut the body of the crab in half and then into quarters. Set aside.

● Put the black beans in a fine-mesh sieve and rinse well to remove the excess salt. Using a mortar and pestle or a cutting board and the back of wooden spoon, crush the beans with the sugar to form a paste. Transfer to small bowl. Whisk in ½ cup (4 fl oz/125 ml) water, the garlic, ginger, chile-garlic sauce, soy sauce, and vinegar until smooth.

● In a large wok or frying pan over medium-high heat, heat the oil. When the oil shimmers, add the crab and stir-fry until heated through, about 5 minutes. Transfer to a platter and keep warm. Reduce the heat to medium and add the black bean mixture. Cook, stirring occasionally, until the sauce is reduced and slightly thickened, 3–5 minutes. Return the crab to the pan and toss to coat well with the sauce.

● Transfer the crab to a warmed platter and pour the sauce over the top. Serve right away, providing seafood crackers and picks at the table.

Simmering, steaming, boiling, and poaching are some of the best ways to cook fish and shellfish quickly while preserving their delicate flavors and textures. In the pages that follow, you will find a versatile recipe for deep-poaching salmon as well as several

Simmered & Steamed

ideas for steaming mussels and clams in a covered pot. You'll also find techniques for "steaming" fish in parchment packets in the oven, which make a dramatic presentation. Finally, two recipes show how to boil fish and shellfish briefly to make a flavorful stew or peel-and-eat meal fit for sharing.

Fish for Simmering & Steaming

Simmering and steaming bring out the best of nearly any type of fin fish and shellfish. In these cooking methods, moisture, in the form of a flavorful liquid or steam, is utilized for cooking. The result is moist, succulent textures and fresh, clean flavors. Often the cooking liquid becomes a rich sauce to enhance the dish.

Preparing & Cooking

Since in some cases you will be serving the cooking liquid with the fish, it is essential to clean all fish, especially shellfish such as clams and mussels, thoroughly (pages 128–32). Pay attention to the cues in the recipes; if the water is simmering too high or too low, it could affect the texture of the cooked fish.

Deep-poaching Fish

This method involves cooking in a large amount of liquid. Be sure the fish is completely submerged so that it cooks evenly. The heat should be low enough so that the liquid shows just a few small bubbles; higher heat may cause the fish to become tough. The cooking liquid will impart flavor to the food, so choose a good-tasting one.

Tips & Tricks

Steaming Fish in Parchment

Tidy packages of parchment are the perfect environment in which to oven-steam small pieces of fish. If you don't have parchment paper you can use aluminum foil, but do not substitute waxed paper, as it cannot withstand the high heat of the oven. Don't worry if your packages don't look pretty—it's more important that they are tightly sealed to capture the hot steam inside.

Steaming Mollusks

A saucepan with a tight-fitting lid is all you need to steam mussels or clams. Try to pull the shellfish out of the pot as soon as the shells open, which is a sign that they are perfectly cooked. Shake the pan often during cooking to encourage the shells to open. Shells that fail to open should be discarded. Be sure to have crusty bread on hand for dipping into the broth.

Boiling & Simmering Fish

When boiling seafood, such as shrimp, squid, or fish pieces, be mindful of the timing and pay attention to the visual cues in the recipes. Boil too long, and you could end up with tough fish. For best results, use a highly flavored cooking liquid to impart flavor to the dish. Clams and mussels still in the shell should not be submerged in liquid, as it will make them tough.

Poaching is one of the best ways to preserve the delicate, silky texture of salmon. And because poaching adds no calories, you can splurge a bit with a classic egg-and-butter hollandaise sauce.

Poached Salmon with Hollandaise

● Pour water to a depth of about 1 inch (2.5 cm) into a saucepan. Have ready a heatproof bowl that fits snugly in the rim of the pan without touching the water below. Bring the water to a boil, then reduce the heat to the lowest setting.

● Off the heat, add the yolks to the bowl. Add ¼ teaspoon salt, the cayenne pepper, and the warm water and whisk until foamy and pale yellow. Set the bowl on the pan and whisk until the yolks become thick and sticky. Pour in about 1 tablespoon of the clarified butter and whisk to blend. Repeat with another tablespoon of the butter. Once the mixture is holding together, whisk in half of the remaining butter in a thin, continuous stream. Whisk in the lemon juice, then slowly whisk in the remaining butter; the mixture will be thick. Taste and adjust the seasonings. Turn off the heat, cover, and set aside.

● Season the fish pieces evenly on both sides with 1 teaspoon salt and ¼ teaspoon white pepper. In a wide saucepan over high heat, warm the fumet. When steam begins to rise from the liquid, reduce the heat to low. Slide the salmon pieces, skinned side down, into the liquid and poach until a skewer easily enters the thickest part of a fillet, about 10 minutes per inch (2.5 cm) of thickness. Transfer to warmed plates, letting each drain briefly.

● Whisk 1–2 tablespoons of the hot poaching liquid into the hollandaise. Spoon the sauce over the fish. Garnish with the chives and serve right away.

3 large egg yolks

Kosher salt and freshly ground white pepper

Pinch of cayenne pepper

1 tbsp warm water

½ cup (4 oz/125 g) Clarified Butter (page 138)

1½ tbsp fresh lemon juice

1 salmon fillet, about 2 lb (1 kg), skinned (page 124) and cut into 6 equal portions (page 125)

6 cups (48 fl oz/1.5 l) Fish Fumet (page 138)

Snipped fresh chives for garnish

MAKES 6 SERVINGS

Watercress's fresh and peppery bite is enhanced by the addition of ginger, garlic, and sesame in this Asian take on pesto. A delicate ginger flavor infuses the salmon and links both elements in the dish.

Salmon with Ginger & Watercress

● In a food processor, process the watercress, olive oil, vegetable oil, sesame oil, sesame seeds, 2 slices of the ginger, one-third of the sliced garlic, and the lemon zest until smooth and bright green. Season to taste and set aside.

● In a large frying pan, heat 1 cup (8 fl oz/250 ml) water, the mirin, lemon juice, and remaining 6 slices of ginger over medium-high heat. When steam begins to rise from the liquid, reduce the heat to medium-low. Slide the salmon fillets into the liquid and sprinkle lightly with salt. Cover the pan tightly and simmer until the salmon is barely opaque in center, about 10 minutes. Remove from the heat and let stand, covered, for 5 minutes.

● Transfer the salmon to a warmed platter, letting each fillet drain briefly. Spread 2 tablespoons of the watercress mixture on top of each fillet and serve right away.

1 bunch watercress, stemmed

¼ cup (2 fl oz/60 ml) extra-virgin olive oil

¼ cup (2 fl oz/60 ml) vegetable oil

2 tsp Asian sesame oil

2 tbsp sesame seeds

Eight ¼-inch (6-mm) slices fresh ginger

3 cloves garlic, thinly sliced

Grated zest of 1 lemon

Kosher salt and freshly ground pepper

¼ cup (2 fl oz/60 ml) mirin

2 tbsp fresh lemon juice

4 thick salmon fillets, each about 6 oz (185 g), skinned

MAKES 4 SERVINGS

Zucchini, cherry tomatoes, and basil are perfect partners for fresh salmon, also available in the summer months. Steaming them in a parchment packet (page 126) lets the natural flavors shine through.

Salmon with Summer Vegetables

2 small zucchini, cut into slivers

Kosher salt and freshly ground pepper

1 salmon fillet (1–1½ lb/500–750 g), skinned, and cut on the diagonal into 4 slices about ¾ inch (2 cm) thick

¼ lb (125 g) cherry tomatoes, stemmed and quartered

8–12 fresh basil leaves

MAKES 6 SERVINGS

- Preheat the oven to 400°F (200°C). Toss the zucchini slivers with 1 teaspoon salt and set aside. Season the salmon with ¼ teaspoon salt and a large pinch of pepper.

- Cut four 12-by-15-inch (30-by-38 cm) sheets of parchment paper. Lay 1 sheet on a work surface, with the long edge facing you, and fold it in half like a book. Use kitchen scissors to cut about 2 inches (5 cm) off each open corner.

- Lay a salmon fillet on the paper about 1 inch (2.5 cm) to the side of the fold on each sheet. Drain off any accumulated liquid from the zucchini and scatter one-fourth of the zucchini slivers on top of each fillet. Divide the cherry tomatoes among the portions and top each with 2 or 3 torn fresh basil leaves.

- For each packet, fold the paper back over the contents, matching the edges. Starting at one end, fold in the corner of the parchment, creasing the fold and creating a new corner. Fold that new corner inward and crease again. Continue folding in a curve around the fish. Twist the end of the packet and place on a rimmed baking sheet.

- Bake until the paper puffs and starts to brown and a skewer easily enters the fish, 7–9 minutes. Transfer the packets to warmed plates. Cut open the packets, slide the contents onto the plates, and serve right away.

Just a few minutes in a pot yields perfectly cooked mussels and a broth full of the bright flavors of wine and fresh parsley. Serve with slices of crusty bread for dipping and soaking.

Mussels with White Wine & Parsley

36 mussels, scrubbed and debearded (page 128)

½ cup (4 fl oz/125 ml) dry white wine

1 shallot, minced

1 tbsp minced fresh flat-leaf parsley

Pinch of freshly ground pepper

1–2 tbsp unsalted butter, optional

Slices of baguette or other crusty French bread for serving

MAKES 3–4 SERVINGS

In a large nonreactive saucepan with a tight-fitting lid, combine the mussels, wine, shallot, parsley, pepper, and butter, if using. Cover the pan and place over high heat. Once steam starts to escape from around the lid, reduce the heat to medium and steam the mussels for about 2 minutes.

After 2 minutes, uncover the pan and check to see how the mussels are cooking. Transfer any opened shells to warmed serving bowls. Re-cover the pan and continue steaming the remaining mussels, stirring and shaking the pan often, until all the mussels are open wide, 1–2 minutes longer. Discard any shells that fail to open after about 8 minutes total cooking time.

Divide the steamed mussels among the serving bowls and ladle some broth into each bowl. Serve right away, passing the bread at the table for dipping into the broth. Set a large bowl in the center of the table to receive empty shells.

There are infinite variations on steamed mussels, as seen in France and Belgium, two nations that specialize in the dish. This Provençal treatment layers anise flavor with both fennel seeds and Pernod.

Mussels with Fennel & Pernod

- Warm a large nonreactive saucepan with a tight-fitting lid over medium heat. Add the olive oil, onion, and garlic and cook, stirring often, until the onion is soft but not browned, about 5 minutes. Add the tomatoes and their juice, the Pernod, and fennel seeds. Raise the heat to high and bring to a boil, uncovered. Add the mussels and cover the pan. Once steam starts to escape from around the lid, reduce the heat to medium and steam the mussels for about 2 minutes.

- After 2 minutes, uncover the pan and check to see how the mussels are cooking. Transfer any opened shells to warmed serving bowls. Re-cover the pan and continue steaming the remaining mussels, stirring and shaking the pan often, until all the mussels are open wide, 1–2 minutes longer. Discard any shells that fail to open after about 8 minutes total cooking time.

- Divide the steamed mussels among the serving bowls and ladle some broth into each bowl. Serve right away, passing the bread at the table for dipping into the broth. Set a large bowl in the center of the table to receive empty shells.

1 tbsp olive oil

½ cup (2 oz/60 g) thinly sliced yellow onion

1 clove garlic, thinly sliced

½ cup (3 oz/90 g) chopped peeled tomatoes (fresh or canned)

2 tbsp Pernod

¼ tsp fennel seeds

36 mussels, scrubbed and debearded (page 128)

Slices of baguette or other crusty French bread for serving

MAKES 3–4 SERVINGS

Hard-shell clams can be used in many recipes that call for mussels. This recipe, based on a Mediterranean tradition, features smoky chorizo to complement the sweet, briny flavor of clams.

Clams with Tomatoes and Sausage

1 oz (30 g) fully cooked Spanish-style chorizo, thinly sliced

½ cup (3 oz/90 g) chopped peeled tomatoes (fresh or canned)

2 tsp chopped fresh flat-leaf parsley

24 small hard-shell clams, such as Manila or littleneck, scrubbed (page 130)

Slices of baguette or other crusty French bread for serving

MAKES 3–4 SERVINGS

- Warm a large, dry saucepan with a tight-fitting lid over medium-low heat. Add the chorizo and cook, turning or stirring occasionally, until the chorizo begins to brown, about 3 minutes. Add the tomatoes with their juice, the parsley, and clams. Cover the pot and raise the heat to high. Once steam starts to escape from the lid, reduce the heat to medium and cook the clams for about 2 minutes.

- After 2 minutes, uncover the pan and check to see how the clams are cooking. Transfer any opened shells to warmed serving bowls. If the tomatoes seem in danger of scorching, add 1–2 tablespoons water. Re-cover the pan and continue steaming the remaining clams, stirring and shaking the pan often, until all the shells are open wide, 1–2 minutes longer. Discard any shells that fail to open after about 8 minutes total cooking time.

- Divide the steamed clams, chorizo, and tomatoes among the serving bowls and ladle some broth into each bowl. Serve right away, passing the bread at the table for dipping into the broth. Set a large bowl in the center of the table to receive empty shells.

Here is a quick version of Bouillabaisse, the famed saffron-scented fish stew of Provence. If you don't have a food mill, use a wooden spoon to push the soup solids through a coarse-mesh sieve.

Seafood Stew

Rouille (page 139)

1 sweet baguette

½ cup (4 fl oz/125 ml) extra-virgin olive oil

1 *each* fennel bulb and onion, thinly sliced

4 cloves garlic

1 can (28 oz/875 g) diced plum tomatoes

Two ½-inch (12-mm) strips orange zest

2 pinches saffron

1 tsp *each* fresh thyme leaves and fennel seeds

6 cups (48 fl oz/1.5 l) Fish Stock (page 138)

Kosher salt and freshly ground pepper

2½ lb (1.25 kg) white fish fillets

1 lb (500 g) *each* large shrimp, hard-shell clams, and mussels

MAKES 6–8 SERVINGS

● Preheat the oven to 350°F (180°C). Make the Rouille according to the recipe. Cut the baguette on the diagonal into 16 slices. Toast the slices in the oven, turning once, until golden, about 10 minutes per side. Set aside.

● In a heavy pot over medium-low heat, heat the oil. When the oil shimmers, add the fennel, onion, and garlic and sauté until softened, about 10 minutes. Stir in the tomatoes with their juice, the orange zest, saffron, thyme, and fennel seeds. Raise the heat to high, add the stock, and bring to a boil. Reduce the heat to low and simmer for 45 minutes.

● Place a food mill fitted with the large grinding disk over a large glass bowl. Ladle the soup base into the mill and turn the crank to force the mixture through. Discard the solids in the mill and return the broth to the pot. Stir in 2 teaspoons salt and ¼ teaspoon pepper.

● Place the broth over medium heat and bring to a boil. Cut the fish into pieces and add to the pan. Reduce the heat to medium, cover, and cook for 5 minutes. Add the shrimp, clams, and mussels. Re-cover and cook until the fish pieces and shrimp are just opaque throughout and the clams and mussels are open, about 3 minutes longer. Remove any unopened shellfish.

● Place 1 or 2 pieces of toasted bread in the bottom of each warmed bowl. Ladle the broth and seafood over the bread. Garnish with the fennel fronds and serve right away, passing the Rouille and any extra bread at the table.

A shrimp boil is a messy, informal, and delicious meal, with everyone peeling their own shrimp by hand at the table. Sweet shrimp, corn, and onions offset the intensely spiced garlic-spiked cooking liquid.

Shrimp Boil with Corn & Potatoes

- Add 8 qt (8 l) water to a large nonreactive stockpot, making sure the water does not fill the pot more than two-thirds full. Add the vinegar, seafood seasoning, 3 tablespoons salt, and the lemon quarters. Cover the pot and bring to a rolling boil over high heat.

- When the water is boiling, add the potatoes, onions, and garlic to the pot, cover, and return to a boil. Reduce the heat to medium and cook until the potatoes are nearly tender when pierced with the tip of a paring knife, about 15 minutes. Add the corn, re-cover, and cook for 5 minutes longer.

- Remove the pot from the heat. Add the shrimp, re-cover, and let stand until the shrimp are bright pink on the outside and opaque throughout, about 5 minutes. Meanwhile, set a large colander in the sink.

- When the shrimp are done, drain the contents of the pot thoroughly in the colander. Discard the lemon and pour the shrimp and vegetables into a large serving bowl. Serve right away, passing the mayonnaise or tartar sauce for dipping the shrimp. Set a large bowl in the center of the table to receive the shrimp shells and corncobs and set out plenty of napkins.

⅓ cup (3 fl oz/ 80 ml) cider vinegar

3 tbsp Chesapeake-style seafood seasoning such as Old Bay

Kosher salt

1 lemon, quartered

2 lb (1 kg) thin-skinned red or white potatoes

1 lb (500 g) yellow onions, sliced

4 cloves garlic

6–8 ears sweet corn, shucked and halved

4 lb (2 kg) head-on or 3 lb (1.5 kg) headless medium shrimp, shells intact

¼ cup (2 fl oz/60 ml) Mayonnaise or Tartar Sauce (page 139), optional

MAKES 6–8 SERVINGS

This recipe shows that red wine can be used for steaming shellfish instead of the expected white wine. For best results, choose a red that is medium-bodied and not too tannic, such as Pinot Noir.

Clams with Red Wine & Thyme

● Put the clams in a large nonreactive saucepan with a tight-fitting lid and add the wine, shallot, thyme, and garlic. Cover the pot and place over high heat. Once steam starts to escape from around the lid, reduce the heat to medium and steam the clams for about 2 minutes.

● After 2 minutes, uncover the pan and check to see how the clams are cooking. Transfer any opened shells to warmed shallow bowls. Re-cover the pan and continue steaming the remaining clams, stirring and shaking the pan often, until all the clams are open wide, 1–2 minutes longer. Discard any shells that fail to open after about 8 minutes total cooking time.

● Divide the steamed clams among the serving bowls and ladle some broth into each bowl. Serve right away, passing the bread at the table for dipping into the broth. Set a large bowl in the center of the table to receive empty shells.

24 small hard-shell clams, such as Manila or littleneck, scrubbed (page 130)

½ cup (4 fl oz/125 ml) dry but fruity red wine

1 shallot, minced

3 or 4 sprigs fresh thyme

1 clove garlic, thinly sliced

Slices of baguette or other crusty French bread for serving

MAKES 3–4 SERVINGS

Quickly steaming clams in a flavorful broth makes a great topping for pasta. Here, the steaming liquid is combined with a generous amount of fruity olive oil and zesty garlic to create the sauce.

Pasta with White Clam Sauce

Kosher salt and freshly ground pepper

⅓ cup (3 fl oz/80 ml) extra-virgin olive oil

3 tbsp minced garlic

1 cup (8 fl oz/250 ml) dry vermouth

2½ pounds hard-shell clams, such as Manila or littleneck, scrubbed (page 130)

1 lb (500 g) dried linguine

2 tbsp minced fresh marjoram

MAKES 6 SERVINGS

● Bring a large pot of generously salted water to a boil over high heat.

● Heat a large frying pan with a tight-fitting lid over medium heat. Add 1 tablespoon of the olive oil, 1 tablespoon of the garlic, and a pinch of salt and sauté until fragrant, about 1 minute. Raise the heat to medium-high, add the vermouth, and simmer until slightly reduced, about 2 minutes. Add the clams, cover the pot tightly, and steam for 4–6 minutes, or until most of the shells have opened wide. Discard any clams that remain tightly shut.

● Place a strainer over a large bowl and pour the clams and their cooking broth through the strainer, reserving the broth. Remove half of the clams from their shells and set them aside.

● When the water comes to a boil, add the linguine and cook until al dente, 7–9 minutes. Drain well.

● In a large frying pan over medium heat, heat the remaining olive oil. Add the remaining 2 tablespoons garlic and cook, stirring constantly, until fragrant, about 1 minute. Add the clam meat, the strained broth, the pasta, half of the marjoram, and a pinch each of salt and pepper and stir to combine.

● Transfer the mixture to a warmed serving bowl, top with the remaining clams in their shells, and the remaining marjoram. Serve right away.

Cooking fish in parchment pouches (page 126) combines the convenience of baking with the delicate touch of moist heat. The fish juices mingle with the herb butter to create an easy sauce.

Snapper with Vegetables & Herb Butter

- Preheat the oven to 400°F (200°C). In a bowl, mix together the butter, parsley, thyme, chives, and a pinch each of salt and pepper. Season the fennel lightly with salt and pepper and toss well.

- Cut four 12-by-15-inch (30-by-38-cm) sheets of parchment paper. Lay 1 sheet on a work surface, with the long edge facing you, and fold it in half like a book. Use kitchen scissors to cut about 2 inches (5 cm) off each open corner.

- Lay a fillet on the paper about 1 inch (2.5 cm) to the side of the fold of each sheet and season it with salt and pepper. Scatter one-fourth each of the fennel and carrot on top, then drizzle with 1 teaspoon of the wine. Spread one-fourth of the herb butter on the opposite side of each fold.

- For each packet, fold the paper back over the contents, matching the edges. Starting at one end, fold in the corner of the parchment, creasing the fold and creating a new corner. Fold that new corner inward and crease again. Continue folding in a curve around the fish. Twist the end of the packet and place on a rimmed baking sheet.

- Bake until the paper puffs and starts to brown and a skewer easily enters the fish, 7–9 minutes.

- Transfer the packets to warmed plates. Cut open the packets, slide the contents onto the plates, and serve right away.

4 tbsp (2 oz/60 g) unsalted butter, at room temperature

2 tsp chopped fresh flat-leaf parsley

1 tsp *each* minced fresh thyme and chives

Kosher salt and freshly ground pepper

4 red snapper, tai snapper, or other firm, lean, mild fish fillets, each 4–6 oz (125–185 g), skinned

2 cups (6 oz/185 g) thinly sliced fennel

1 large carrot, cut into matchsticks

4 tsp dry white wine

MAKES 4 SERVINGS

Greeks have known for centuries that tender shrimp is delicious when paired with ripe summer tomatoes and tangy feta cheese. The addition of ouzo lends a complementary anise flavor.

Shrimp with Tomatoes, Fennel & Feta

- Bring a large pot of water to a boil over medium-high heat. Add 1 tablespoon salt and the shrimp and boil until the shrimp are just opaque, about 2 minutes. Drain and plunge into a bowl of ice water to stop the cooking. Drain well and pat dry.

- In a large bowl, whisk together ½ teaspoon salt, the vinegar, ouzo, and garlic until the salt is dissolved. Whisk in ¼ teaspoon pepper, the oil, oregano, and parsley to make a dressing. Add the shrimp to the dressing along with the fennel, tomatoes, and feta cheese. Toss to mix, taste, and adjust the seasonings. Cover and refrigerate for 1 hour before serving.

- Just before serving, taste again and adjust the seasonings. Arrange a handful of arugula leaves on each of 4 plates and top with the shrimp, vegetables, and cheese. Serve right away.

Kosher salt and freshly ground pepper

1 lb (500 g) large shrimp, peeled and deveined

¼ cup (2 fl oz/60 ml) white wine vinegar

3 tbsp ouzo

2 cloves garlic, minced

⅓ cup (3 fl oz/80 ml) extra-virgin olive oil

1 tsp minced fresh oregano

1 tbsp minced fresh flat-leaf parsley

1 fennel bulb, very thinly sliced

1 pint grape tomatoes, halved

6 oz (185 g) feta cheese, cut into cubes

2 cups arugula leaves

MAKES 4 SERVINGS

This salad is redolent of garlic, capers, and olives. Velvety white beans give it body and texture. Finally, roasted peppers and red onion add color and flavor to this intriguing main-course salad.

Calamari & White Bean Salad

Kosher salt and freshly ground pepper

1 lb (500 g) squid bodies, cut into thin rings (page 131)

1 can (14.5 oz/455 g) cannellini beans

¼ cup (2 fl oz/60 ml) white wine vinegar

3 tbsp fresh lemon juice

1 tbsp minced garlic

½ cup (4 fl oz/125 ml) extra-virgin olive oil

1 *each* red and yellow bell pepper, roasted (page 138), peeled, and cut into strips

1 cup (3½ oz/105 g) thinly sliced red onion

2 tbsp capers

⅓ cup (2 oz/60 g) green olives, chopped

MAKES 4 SERVINGS

● In a large pot, bring 4 qt (4 l) water to a rolling boil over high heat. Add 1 tablespoon salt along with the squid and cook until just tender, about 1 minute. (The water will stop boiling.) Drain the squid and plunge into a bowl of ice water to stop the cooking. Drain well and pat dry.

● Rinse the beans under cold running water. Drain well and pat dry.

● In a large bowl, combine ¼ cup (2 fl oz/60 ml) vinegar, the lemon juice, 1 teaspoon salt, ¼ teaspoon pepper, and the garlic and let stand for 5 minutes. Whisk in the olive oil to make a dressing.

● Add the cooked calamari, white beans, roasted peppers, onion, capers, and olives to the dressing and mix well. Cover and refrigerate for at least 2 hours to develop the flavors.

● Just before serving, taste the salad and adjust the vinegar and seasonings. Divide among serving plates and serve right away.

Cooking fish in the dry heat of an oven brings out the natural flavors and textures of the fish. In this chapter you'll find a handful of recipes for roasting fish on the bone. Though it may seem daunting at first, this technique is actually fairly easy and makes

Roasted & Baked

a dramatic presentation. There is also a recipe in which the whole fish bakes in a dome of salt, which locks in the natural juices as the fish cooks. You will find several simple ideas for roasting thick, meaty fish fillets and one for pan-roasting clams, any of which make a great option for a delicious meal.

Fish for Roasting & Baking

More than any other cooking method, roasting and baking are perfect for cooking whole fish, such as striped bass, snapper, and trout, among others. Thick fish fillets and steaks also do well in the hot, dry heat of the oven where thin fillets would easily overcook. Shellfish are delicious when tucked in with roasting vegetables.

Preparing to Cook

Rinse the fish well and pat completely dry with paper towels; a surface free of moisture will encourage browning. Season the fish just before roasting to bring out the natural flavors. Many recipes call for coating the fish with oil before roasting, which both protects the fish from the oven's heat and promotes even browning.

Controlling the Heat

Preheat the oven for at least 15 minutes, especially when roasting at 400°F (200°C) and above. If your oven does not seem hot enough, use an oven thermometer to test its accuracy and then adjust the temperature gauge up or down to compensate. Manage any hot spots in your oven by turning the pan halfway through cooking.

Tips & Tricks

Working with Whole Fish

The fishmonger will generally sell whole fish that is already gutted, scaled, and cleaned, but it's a good idea to clean it again when you get home. Check the fish for any errant scales and scrape them off (page 122). Rinse the fish well inside and out to remove any remaining blood or viscera; pat very dry. Season the fish inside and out to ensure fully flavored fish.

About Skin & Bones

Keeping the skin and bones intact, as shown in many of these recipes, preserves the natural flavors and moisture during cooking. The skin is easily pulled off after cooking for diners who don't care to eat it, but many enjoy the crisp texture that it gains after roasting. Warn guests of the possibility of encountering bones in both fish steaks and whole fish.

Roasting Shellfish

Shellfish are well suited to roasting over high temperatures. To ensure even cooking, select shells that are about the same size. Clean the shellfish well (pages 127–30) and discard any shells that fail to close to the touch. After cooking, remove and discard any shells that did not open during the cooking process. When serving, set out a bowl to collect the discarded shells.

Roasting preserves a whole fish's moisture and flavor. Here, mushrooms and leeks add a subtle earthy scent, and their juices mingle with those from the fish to create a natural sauce.

Striped Bass with Vegetables

- In a small bowl, combine 1 teaspoon salt and ¼ teaspoon pepper and rub all but about ⅛ teaspoon of the mixture evenly over the fish, inside and out.

- Brush a long baking dish with a little olive oil. Line the dish with a layer of the dark green parts of the leeks and add the fish. If the tail hangs over the edge, wrap it loosely in aluminum foil.

- Preheat the oven to 400°F (200°C). In a frying pan over medium heat, melt the butter. Add the light parts of the leeks and half of the reserved salt-pepper mixture and sauté until softened and light gold, about 10 minutes. Using a slotted spoon, lift out the leeks and spread over and around the fish. Add the mushrooms and remaining salt-pepper mixture to the pan, raise the heat to medium-high, and sauté until the mushrooms begin to brown, about 5 minutes. Pour the contents of the pan over the fish.

- Roast the fish in the oven until an instant-read thermometer inserted into the thickest part of the fish registers 125°F (52°C), about 25 minutes.

- Carve the fish (page 137) and serve right away on warmed plates with the vegetables and cooking juices.

Kosher salt and freshly ground pepper

1 large whole striped bass, about 4 lb (2 kg), gutted and scaled by the fishmonger

Olive oil

3 large leeks, white and pale green parts cut into 1-inch (2.5-cm) pieces and dark green parts cut into 3-inch (7.5 cm) lengths

2 tbsp unsalted butter

¾ lb (375 g) brown or white button mushrooms, thickly sliced

MAKES 6 SERVINGS

Fresh sardines take well to roasting and, like other strong-flavored fish, are delicious with assertive herbs such as rosemary. This dish might change your opinion about those little fish in cans.

Sardines with Rosemary Butter

- In a bowl, beat together the rosemary, butter, lemon zest, and a pinch each of salt and pepper. Cover and refrigerate.

- Preheat the oven to 400°F (200°C). Fill a large bowl three-fourths full of cold water, keeping track of how many cups you have added, and stir in 1 tablespoon salt per cup (8 fl oz/250 ml) of water. Add the cleaned sardines and rub off any scales under the water. Set aside.

- Coat a large baking dish with olive oil. Scatter the sliced onion in the dish. Drain the sardines, pat dry, and arrange in a single layer on top of the onions. Sprinkle with a large pinch of pepper.

- Remove the rosemary butter from the refrigerator. Roast the sardines until the meat shrinks noticeably from the ribs, about 15 minutes.

- Serve the fish right away, passing the rosemary butter at the table for spooning over the top. At the table, show diners how to bone each fish with a knife and fork; it's the same basic procedure as carving a whole fish (page 137), but the smallest bones are edible.

1 tbsp chopped fresh rosemary

4 tbsp (2 oz/60 g) unsalted butter, at room temperature

Grated zest of 1 lemon

Kosher salt and freshly ground pepper

1½–2 lb (750 g–1 kg) fresh sardines, gutted and cleaned by the fishmonger

Olive oil

1 small yellow onion, thinly sliced

MAKES 6 SERVINGS

Monkfish is buttery rich, resembling lobster in flavor. Here, it's roasted along with a trio of fresh vegetables and a duo of fresh herbs to make a delicious one-pan sauce for short pasta tubes.

Monkfish with Pasta & Tomatoes

2 pt (12 oz/375 g) grape tomatoes

2 cloves garlic, minced

1 yellow onion, thinly sliced

4 tbsp (2 fl oz/60 ml) olive oil

Kosher salt and freshly ground pepper

4 monkfish fillets, each about 6 oz (185 g)

1 tbsp balsamic vinegar

¼ cup chopped fresh flat-leaf parsley

2 tbsp chopped fresh basil

¾ cup (6 fl oz/180 ml) dry vermouth

8 oz (250 g) dried penne rigate pasta

MAKES 4 SERVINGS

● Preheat the oven to 425°F (220°C). In a roasting pan, combine the tomatoes, garlic, onion, 2 tablespoons of the olive oil, ½ teaspoon salt, and a few grinds of pepper. Toss to coat well. Roast until they begin to soften and brown around the edges, about 25 minutes.

● Pat the fish dry with paper towels and season with ¼ teaspoon salt and pepper to taste. In a small bowl, combine ¼ teaspoon salt with the vinegar and whisk to dissolve the salt. Add the remaining 2 tablespoons olive oil and whisk to combine.

● Remove the pan from the oven and lay the monkfish on top of the vegetables. Pour the vinegar mixture over the top and sprinkle with the parsley and half of the basil. Pour the vermouth around the fish and return the pan to the oven. Roast until the fish is cooked through and firm to the touch, 12–15 minutes.

● Meanwhile, bring a large pot of generously salted water to a boil. Cook the pasta according the package directions, then drain and keep warm.

● Transfer the fish to a warmed plate, then use the back of a fork to smash the vegetables to make a chunky sauce. Taste and adjust the seasonings.

● Divide the cooked pasta among 4 warmed shallow bowls and top with the vegetables and their juices and a monkfish fillet. Sprinkle with the remaining basil and serve right away.

Roasting whole fish in a dome of salt creates a dense golden crust that locks in the natural juices as the fish cooks. A mayonnaise-based sauce seasoned with garlic is the perfect finish.

Salt-Roasted Fish

1 large whole snapper, tai snapper or striped bass, 3–4 lb (1.5–2 kg) total weight, gutted by the fishmonger, with the scales left on

Freshly ground pepper

3 or 4 thin lemon slices

3 or 4 sprigs fresh flat-leaf parsley

6 cups (about 1½ lb/ 750 g) kosher salt

3 egg whites, lightly beaten

½ cup (4 fl oz/125 ml) Aioli (page 139)

MAKES 6 SERVINGS

• Preheat the oven to 400°F (200°C). Measure the thickness of the fish and make a note of the figure. Season the fish inside and out with ¼ teaspoon pepper and tuck 3 lemon slices and 3 parsley sprigs in the cavity.

• Choose an oval baking dish that is about 1 inch (2.5 cm) larger than the fish. In a large bowl, stir together the salt and egg whites until evenly moistened. Spread a ¼-inch (6-mm) layer of the mixture in the dish and place the fish on top. Using your hands, spread the rest of the salt in an even layer all over the fish, pressing so it adheres to the salt on the bottom of the dish. If any gaps appear in the coating, fill them in with more dry salt, cementing it into place with a few drops of water.

• Place the fish in the oven and roast for 12 minutes per 1 inch (2.5 cm) of thickness. Remove from the oven. Insert an instant-read thermometer through the crust near the head end. The fish is done if the thermometer registers 115°F (46°C). If it's not done yet, return the fish to the oven for 3–5 minutes longer and test again.

• Use 2 metal serving spoons to crack the crust and lift it away in large pieces, setting them on a plate. The skin may come away with the crust; if not, peel it back with the spoons. Carve the fish (page 137) and serve right away. Pass the Aioli at the table.

Here, earthy morel mushrooms and smoky bacon give mild-flavored cod a burst of flavor. Just a touch of Champagne vinegar and a spoonful of fresh chives lend freshness to brighten the dish.

Cod with Bacon & Morels

- Preheat the oven to 375°F (190°C). Soak the mushrooms in the boiling water until softened, about 20 minutes. Drain, squeeze dry, and roughly chop into bite-sized pieces. Set aside.

- In a large ovenproof frying pan, melt 2 tablespoons of the butter over medium-high heat. Add the bacon and cook until crisp, about 3 minutes. Transfer to a paper towel–lined plate.

- Pour off all but 3 tablespoons of the fat in the pan and add the leeks and ¼ teaspoon salt. Sauté until tender and beginning to brown, about 10 minutes. Crumble half the bacon and add it to the leeks along with the reserved mushrooms and vinegar. Toss well and spread the mixture out over the bottom of the pan.

- Lightly season the fish with salt and pepper and lay on top of the leeks. Dot with the remaining 1 tablespoon butter. Roast until the fish flakes easily when prodded with a fork, about 12 minutes.

- Serve the fish on warmed plates with a spoonful of the vegetable mixture on the side. Crumble the remaining bacon over the top and garnish with the chives.

¾ ounce (20 g) dried morel mushrooms

½ cup (4 fl oz/125 ml) boiling water

3 tbsp unsalted butter

4 slices thick-cut bacon

2 cups (6 oz/180 g) thinly sliced leeks, white and light green parts only

Kosher salt and freshly ground pepper

1 tsp Champagne vinegar

4 cod fillets, each about 6 oz (185 g)

1 tbsp snipped fresh chives

MAKES 4 SERVINGS

Firm-fleshed red snapper, one of the most popular varieties of white fish, stands up well to strong flavorings. In this dish, bright cilantro and lime combine with spices for a vinaigrette-style sauce.

Snapper with Cilantro & Lime

1 whole red snapper,
about 4 lb (2 kg),
or two 2-lb (1-kg)
snappers, cleaned
and scaled

Kosher salt and freshly
ground pepper

1 bunch fresh cilantro

6–8 thin lime slices

Olive oil

1 small white onion,
thinly sliced

3 tbsp fresh lime juice

½ tsp ground cumin

¼ tsp ground ginger

MAKES 6 SERVINGS

- Preheat the oven to 400°F (200°C). Lightly season the fish inside and out with salt and pepper.

- Chop 3 tablespoons of the leaves from the cilantro bunch and set aside. Stuff the remaining cilantro sprigs and the lime slices inside the cavity of the fish.

- Coat a large baking dish with olive oil and scatter the onion in the dish. Lay the fish on top of the onions and roast until an instant-read thermometer inserted into the thickest part of the fish registers 125°F (52°C), 18–20 minutes.

- While the fish is roasting, whisk together the lime juice, ¾ teaspoon salt, the cumin, ginger, and a pinch of pepper. Stir in ¼ cup (2 fl oz/60 ml) olive oil and the reserved chopped cilantro to make a sauce.

- Carve the fish (page 137), place on warmed plates, and serve right away with the sauce on the side.

Consider this a salmon "roast," the perfect option for easy entertaining. Here, a chunky olive-caper mixture makes a fragrant stuffing and negates the need for a separate sauce.

Salmon with Olives & Capers

- Preheat the oven to 400°F (200°C). Choose a baking dish that will hold the folded salmon snugly and rub it with the olive oil. Lay the fish in the dish, unfold it, and season the inside with the ¼ teaspoon pepper.

- On a large cutting board, pile the garlic, anchovy fillets, capers, and olives. Chop everything together until the ingredients are thoroughly combined but the mixture is still somewhat chunky. Spread the olive mixture evenly on the bottom inside half of the fish and fold the other side over into its original position. Tie the fish with kitchen string in several places to ensure it roasts evenly.

- Roast the fish, uncovered, until an instant-read thermometer inserted into the thickest part of the fish registers 115°F (46°C), 30–35 minutes. Meanwhile, toss the zucchini ribbons with a pinch each of salt and pepper. Add the zucchini to the dish alongside the fish during the last 10 minutes of roasting.

- Cut the fish crosswise into 6 equal sections and serve right away with some of the zucchini on warmed plates.

1 salmon roast, 3 lb (1.5 kg), skin on, scaled, and boned

Scant 1 tbsp olive oil

Freshly ground pepper

1 clove garlic, minced

2 rinsed and dried canned anchovy fillets

1 tbsp rinsed and drained capers

¾ cup (3 oz/90 g) pitted Kalamata olives

4 zucchini, cut lengthwise into thin ribbons with a vegetable peeler

MAKES 6 SERVINGS

"Butterflied" trout is a convenient cut of fish. It's deboned, but held together in one piece by the skin, ideal for stuffing. Here, its mild flavor gets a lift from a horseradish-spiked bread-crumb mixture.

Trout with Horseradish Stuffing

- Preheat the oven to 400°F (200°C). In a small bowl, stir together the mayonnaise, parsley, green onion, and horseradish.

- Coat a large oval baking dish with olive oil. Season the insides of the fish with ½ teaspoon salt and a large pinch of pepper. Working with one fish at a time, spread one-sixth of the horseradish mixture all over the inside of the fish. Sprinkle the bread crumbs over the horseradish mixture, dividing it evenly, and fold the fish back together. Arrange the trout in the dish.

- Roast, uncovered, until an instant-read thermometer inserted into the thickest part of the fish registers 115°F (46°C), 12–15 minutes. Serve right away on warmed plates.

3 tbsp Mayonnaise (page 139)

2 tbsp minced fresh flat-leaf parsley

2 tbsp minced green onion

1½ tsp prepared horseradish

Olive oil

6 small butterflied boneless trout, each about ½ lb (250 g), cleaned

Kosher salt and freshly ground pepper

6 tbsp fine dried bread crumbs

MAKES 6 SERVINGS

Arctic char is a relative of both salmon and trout, and can be substituted for either fish in recipes. The oily, herb-spiked brine from marinated artichoke hearts works beautifully as a marinade.

Arctic Char with Artichokes & Lemon

1 whole Arctic char, 3–4 lb (1.5–2 kg), cleaned and scaled

Kosher salt and freshly ground pepper

1 large lemon

2 jars (6½ oz/200 g each) marinated artichoke hearts

MAKES 6 SERVINGS

Preheat the oven to 400°F (200°C). Season the fish inside the cavity and on the outside with ½ teaspoon salt and ⅛ teaspoon pepper.

Using a vegetable peeler, remove the zest from the lemon in strips, avoiding the white pith, then cut the zest into ribbons ⅛ inch (3 mm) wide. Slice off the ends of the lemon, stand it upright, cut away the pith, and cut then cut the flesh crosswise into slices ¼ inch (6 mm) thick.

Pour the marinated artichokes into a bowl. Spoon 2 tablespoons of the marinade into a large baking dish. Lay the fish in the dish and tuck half of the lemon slices in the fish cavity. Scatter the artichoke hearts and lemon zest slivers around the fish, drizzle another 1 tablespoon of the marinade over the fish, and lay the remaining lemon slices on top.

Roast, uncovered, until an instant-read thermometer inserted into the thickest part of the fish registers 115°F (46°C), 30–35 minutes. Discard the lemon slices.

Carve the fish (page 137) and divide among warmed plates along with the artichokes and lemon zest. Serve right away.

Tart tomatillos dress up crisp potatoes and halibut fillets. Flavored with cilantro, onion, garlic, lime, and hot serrano chiles, the Latin-style green sauce is a great way to offset these mild ingredients.

Halibut & Potatoes with Green Salsa

12 oz (375 g) fingerling potatoes

3 tbsp olive oil

Kosher salt and freshly ground pepper

Tomatillo Salsa, page 139

4 halibut fillets, each about 6 oz (185 g)

Chopped fresh cilantro for garnish

MAKES 4 SERVINGS

● Preheat the oven to 425°F (220°C). Cut the potatoes in half lengthwise and spread them out on a rimmed baking sheet. Drizzle with 1 tablespoon of the oil and season with salt and pepper. Roast until browned and almost crisp, about 20 minutes.

● While the potatoes cook, heat the remaining 2 tablespoons oil in a large frying pan and add the salsa. Cook until slightly thickened, about 5 minutes. Remove from the heat, taste, and adjust the seasonings. Keep warm.

● Lightly season the fillets with salt. Lay them on the baking sheet with the potatoes, pushing the potatoes to the side as needed. Roast until the fish is cooked through, 10–12 minutes.

● Transfer the potatoes and fish to a warmed platter and pour the tomatillo salsa over the top. Garnish with cilantro and serve right away.

Mackerel's strong flavor is tamed when topped with a compound butter flavored with whole-grain mustard and fresh tarragon. Serve with mashed potatoes or celery root to soak up the flavorful sauce.

Mackerel with Mustard Butter

● Preheat the oven to 400°F (200°C). Heat a small frying pan over medium heat and add 1 tablespoon of the butter. When the butter sizzles, add the shallots and sauté until translucent, about 1 minute. Transfer to a small bowl. Add 4 tablespoons of the butter, the mustard, tarragon, ¼ teaspoon salt, and a pinch each of pepper and cayenne and blend together with a fork. Scrape the butter mixture onto a sheet of plastic wrap and refrigerate until slightly firm, about 30 minutes. Roll the butter into a log about 1 inch (2.5 cm) thick, wrap in plastic wrap, and refrigerate for at least 30 minutes until firm.

● Heat a large ovenproof frying pan over medium-high heat and add the remaining 1 tablespoon butter. Lightly season the fillets with ¼ teaspoon salt and a pinch of pepper. Add the fillets to the hot frying pan and cook until lightly browned, about 1 minute. Turn the fillets and transfer the pan to the oven. Roast the fish until cooked through, about 3 minutes.

● Divide the fillets among warmed serving plates. Cut thin rounds from the chilled butter log and place on top of the fish. Serve right away.

6 tbsp unsalted butter, at room temperature

3 tbsp minced shallots

1 tbsp whole-grain mustard

1 tbsp minced fresh tarragon

Salt and freshly ground black pepper

Pinch of cayenne pepper

4 mackerel or bluefish fillets, about 6 oz (185 g) each

MAKES 4 SERVINGS

This one-dish recipe offers tender red potatoes, licorice-tinged fennel, toasty garlic, and briny clams. Spicy red pepper flakes and dry white wine mix with the clam's juices to create a flavorful sauce.

Pan-Roasted Clams & Vegetables

2 lb (1 kg) small red potatoes, quartered

1 fennel bulb, cut into slices ¼ inch (6 mm) thick, some of the fronds reserved for garnish

5 cloves garlic, roughly chopped

¼ cup (2 fl oz/60 ml) extra-virgin olive oil

Kosher salt and freshly ground black pepper

4 lb (2 kg) littleneck clams, about 40, scrubbed (page 130)

½ tsp red pepper flakes

¼ cup (2 fl oz/60 ml) dry white wine

MAKES 4 SERVINGS

● Preheat the oven to 475°F (245°C). Heat a large flameproof roasting pan on the stove top over medium-high heat. Add the potatoes, fennel, garlic, olive oil, 1 teaspoon salt, and ¼ teaspoon pepper. Cook, stirring occasionally, until the vegetables begin to soften, about 5 minutes, and transfer the pan to the oven. Roast until the potatoes are browned, about 20 minutes.

● Add the clams and red pepper flakes to the pan, and cover tightly with aluminum foil. Roast, covered, giving the ingredients a stir halfway through cooking time, until the clams have opened, about 15 minutes. Pour in the wine, re-cover, and let stand for 1 minute to blend the flavors.

● Discard any clams that haven't opened, then divide the clams, vegetables, and cooking juices among warmed serving bowls. Garnish the bowls with fennel fronds and serve right away.

This simple dish shines with fresh tomatoes, garlic, and herbs, iconic ingredients of southern France. Prepare it when you don't have the time for an elaborate dish, but still aim to impress your guests.

Fish Provençal

- Preheat the oven to 375°F (190°C). Lightly oil a baking dish just large enough to hold the fillets snugly in a single layer.

- Place the fillets in the prepared baking dish, season lightly with salt and pepper, and drizzle with the wine. Arrange the tomato slices on top of the fish, overlapping them slightly if necessary. In a small bowl, stir together 2 tablespoons of the olive oil, the garlic, tarragon, parsley, and thyme. Spoon the herb mixture evenly over the tomatoes, season with more salt and pepper to taste, and sprinkle with the bread crumbs. Drizzle with the remaining 1 tablespoon olive oil.

- Bake until the bread crumbs are browned on top and the fish is opaque throughout, 25–30 minutes. Serve right away, directly from the baking dish.

4 halibut fillets,
6–8 oz (185–250 g) each

Kosher salt and freshly
ground pepper

2 tbsp dry white wine

1 lb (500 g) ripe
tomatoes, cut into
slices ½ inch (12 mm)
thick

3 tbsp extra-virgin
olive oil

1 clove garlic, minced

1 tbsp *each* chopped
fresh tarragon and
flat-leaf parsley

¼ tsp fresh thyme
leaves

2–3 tbsp fine dried
bread crumbs

MAKES 4 SERVINGS

Belgian endive serves as a natural roasting rack for the snapper fillets in this recipe. Its slight bitterness, which softens during cooking, complements the mildness of the fish.

Snapper Fillets with Belgian Endive

- Preheat the oven to 450°F (230°C). Cut each endive in half lengthwise, then cut out and discard the hard core. Slice the halves lengthwise into wedges about ½ inch (12 mm) wide and add to a shallow baking dish just large enough to hold the fish. Drizzle the melted butter over the endive wedges, season lightly with salt and pepper, and toss to coat. Roast for 10 minutes.

- Remove the dish from the oven and turn over the endive wedges. Add the broth, vinegar, and sugar and continue to roast for another 10 minutes.

- Meanwhile, pat dry the fillets. Lightly brush or rub both sides with olive oil, then season both sides lightly with salt and pepper.

- Remove the dish from the oven and place the fillets on top of the endive wedges. Roast until the fish is opaque throughout and the endive is tender, 8–10 minutes.

- Divide the endive and fish among warmed individual plates and serve right away.

6–8 heads Belgian endive, 12–14 oz (375–440 g) total weight

2 tbsp unsalted butter, melted

Kosher salt and freshly ground pepper

¼ cup (2 fl oz/60 ml) reduced-sodium chicken broth

1 tbsp sherry vinegar

½ tsp sugar

2 red snapper fillets, 10–12 oz (315–375 g) each, skinned

Extra-virgin olive oil

MAKES 4 SERVINGS

This recipe takes advantage of summer's delicious bounty, featuring ripe tomatoes, zucchini, and fresh basil. Shop at the farmers' market and you may also be able to pick up fish from the local fish purveyor.

Cod Baked with Zucchini & Tomato

1 lb (500 g) Yukon gold potatoes, unpeeled

2 tbsp olive oil

2 lb (500 g) cod fillets, skin intact

Kosher salt and freshly ground pepper

1 ripe tomato, cut into ¼ inch (6 mm) slices

1 zucchini, cut into ¼ inch (6 mm) diagonal slices

1 small yellow onion, sliced

2 tbsp chopped fresh basil

MAKES 6 SERVINGS

● In a saucepan of boiling water, cook the whole potatoes until tender, about 20 minutes. Drain and let cool. Peel and cut into slices ¼ inch (6 mm) thick.

● Preheat the oven to 400°F (200°C). Choose a baking dish that will hold the fillets in a single layer and brush with ½ tablespoon of the oil. Lay the fillets, skin side down, in the prepared dish. Sprinkle lightly with salt and pepper. Arrange the potato slices in overlapping rows on top of the fish. Create a row of tomato and zucchini slices down the middle, alternating the vegetables. Scatter the onion over the top and drizzle with the remaining 1½ tablespoons oil. Season the vegetables lightly with salt and pepper.

● Bake until the fish is opaque throughout, about 35 minutes. Remove from the oven, sprinkle with the chopped basil, and serve right away, directly from the dish.

Types of Fish & Shellfish

Sorting out the hundreds of varieties of edible fish is a fascinating study in natural history. But for many, the most important thing to know is the best way to cook the fish to enhance its texture and flavor.

Each type of fish and shellfish has a unique combination of characteristics that define the flavor, texture, and best cooking methods. The texture of seafood can range from firm and dense to light and delicate. Flavors can range from mild and sweet to strong and distinctive. And the fat content also varies from lean and flaky to rich and oily. These qualities make each fish or shellfish better suited to certain cooking methods than others. As always, speak to your fishmonger; a good one will help you select the best type of fish or shellfish for the recipe you are preparing.

For Roasting, Grilling & Broiling
The dry heat of a grill, broiler, or oven is best for meaty-textured "steak fish," such as swordfish, tuna, and halibut, which contain a moderate to high fat content. This preparation is also ideal for just about any whole fish, from small, fresh sardines to meaty striped bass.

For Steaming & Poaching
Poaching, or cooking in barely simmering liquid, is the gentlest cooking method, perfect for nearly any type of fish that you enjoy eating with a tender, delicate texture. Steaming in a closed pot is the classic way to cook such bivalves as clams and mussels. Crustaceans (such as crab, lobster, and shrimp) are often boiled whole, in the shell. For the best results, keep the water at a gentle, rather than rolling, boil.

Almost any fish fillets or small pieces of lean to moderately rich fish, including snapper, halibut, or salmon, or shellfish, such as shrimp or scallops, can be baked in a parchment paper pouch, where they "steam" in the moisture that collects in the parchment packet.

For Sautéing & Frying
Most types of fish are suitable for sautéing, especially thin fillets like sole, flounder, tilapia, or trout, which develop a crunchy crust after cooking in the hot oil. Pan-seared scallops and sweet shrimp cook quickly and stay juicy and tender in a hot sauté pan.

For deep-frying, you'll want thicker fish fillets that have some body, and can be cut into pieces; cod is the classic example, and most similarly-shaped, firm white fish, such as halibut, are also suitable.

Shrimp, cut-up squid, scallops, and other firm shellfish are also ideal for dredging in batter or breadcrumbs and deep-frying.

Fish & Shellfish Glossary

As the adage goes, there are many fish in the sea. The following species appear in this book, each with its unique flavor and texture.

Arctic Char A cousin to salmon, caught in cold waters. Light, flaky, delicate-flavored flesh.

Catfish A fairly firm, white-fleshed freshwater fish from the American South. Best pan-fried.

Clams Saltwater mollusks that range in size from small littlenecks to large surfs. When fresh they are plump, juicy, and nutty-sweet.

Cod A mild and lean saltwater fish, with familiar white flesh. Avoid grilling, due to its flakiness. Pollock is a flavorful substitute.

Crab Popular varieties of this saltwater crustacean include blue, Dungeness, and king. They yield sweet, milky, tender meat.

Flounder An Atlantic flatfish which may masquerade as sole. Lean and delicate flesh that requires quick cooking by any method.

Halibut A large flatfish from cold waters. Its firm white flesh is exceedingly versatile.

Mackerel Oily, flavorful, tender saltwater fish. Wonderful roasted or grilled.

Mahimahi A tropical, warm water fish, with dense, sweet pink flesh and moderate fat content. A great candidate for grilling.

Monkfish A white-fleshed saltwater fish, sometimes called "the poor man's lobster" for its meaty texture and mild, sweet flavor.

Mussels A saltwater mollusk with cream- to orange-colored meat that is sweeter than that of oysters or clams. Pleasantly chewy.

Oysters The most tender mollusk, sweet and briny in flavor. Colder waters develop a firmer texture and sharper, saltier flavor, while warmer waters create a softer, milder oyster.

Salmon A beautifully textured, oil rich, pink-fleshed fish with a distinct flavor.

Sardines Small, slim, oily saltwater fish. Excellent roasted or grilled.

Scallops The firmest mollusk, plump, sweet, and flavorful. Bay scallops are smaller and more tender than sea scallops, but milder.

Sea Bass This family includes groupers, black bass, striped bass, blue-nose bass, and white sea bass. Very fine, tender, moist white flesh suitable to many cooking methods.

Shrimp The main varieties include Gulf shrimp, tiger shrimp, and Monterey prawns, varying in sizes and colors.

Skate White, lean flesh comes from the wings of this flat-shaped animal.

Snapper A firm and lean saltwater fish. Popular varieties are red and yellowtail. West Coast rockfish commonly substitutes.

Sole A slim, delicate ocean flatfish. Common varieties are Dover, lemon, petrale, and rex. Sauté or poach the delicate fillets with care.

Squid An inexpensive and delicious fish, also called calamari. Has a sweet, mild flavor. Pleasantly firm bite. Rubbery if overcooked.

Swordfish A giant, warm water ocean fish, always sold as a chunk or steak. It has firm, richly-flavored white flesh.

Tilapia A commonly farmed Latin American freshwater fish, lean and very mild.

Trout A clean tasting, sweet-scented river fish. Delicate and somewhat oily.

Tuna Meaty saltwater fish. Colors range from white to dark red flesh. Grill or roast.

SUSTAINABLE SEAFOOD

The resources of the world's oceans were once thought to be limitless, but today we know that some types of seafood are struggling for survival. Dedicated organizations caution against buying certain species due to overfishing, unregulated fishing, or harmful farming practices. Ask your retailer or fishmonger if he or she is confident that the shop's fish comes from trusted sources.

Several watch groups and ocean advocacy organizations have websites that are devoted to seafood sustainability, and publish comprehensive lists on endangered species, the best choices of fish or seafood for eating, and contamination issues. Two excellent watch groups are the Monterey Bay Aquarium's Seafood Watch program (www.mbayaq.org), and the Environmental Defense Fund's Seafood Selector guide (www.edf.org).

Contrary to what you might think, farm-raised seafood is not always a good choice. According to some authorities, aquacultured fish actually do more harm than good to the environment. As with naturally-raised fish and shellfish, educate yourself about the foods you are eating and ask a lot of questions in order to be sure you are making the best choice for both yourself and the planet.

Cleaning a Whole Gutted & Scaled Fish

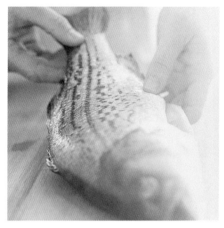

1 Inspect the fish
You can buy a whole fish that has been gutted and scaled, or dressed, by the fishmonger, but it may need further cleaning. Look for gills, fins, stray scales, and blood or entrails inside, and remove.

2 Trim the sharp fins, if present
Lay the fish on one side. Using a boning knife or a paring knife, make shallow ½-inch (12-mm) incisions next to the fins on both the upper side (dorsal fin) and the lower or belly side (anal fin).

3 Remove the fins
Using fish tweezers, needle-nose pliers, or a kitchen towel, firmly pull the fins away along with the supporting bones. Repeat steps 2 and 3, if necessary, to remove the fins on the other side of the fish.

4 Remove any stray scales
Using the back of a stiff knife, scrape away any stray scales, running the knife from the tail end toward the head. You may want to do this in a large bag or sink to keep the scales from scattering.

5 Scrape away any blood inside
Open the fish cavity. With the tip of the boning or paring knife, slit open the membrane along the backbone inside the cavity (the kidney strip). Scrape and rinse out any traces of blood or entrails.

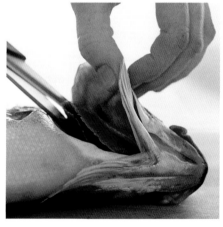

6 Snip the gills and rinse the fish
If the gills, which look like pink or red crescents on the sides of the fish, are still present, snip them out with kitchen scissors. Rinse the fish well inside and out under running cold water and pat it dry.

Filleting a Whole Fish

1 Cut below the head
After cleaning the fish as directed at left, separate the flesh from the head on one side. With the head pointing away from you, and using a fillet knife, make a diagonal cut halfway through the fish just below the gill.

2 Cut along the back
Starting at the fish's head, run the knife along the back near the backbone, cutting through the skin and into the flesh about 1 inch (2.5 cm) deep until you reach the tail and can see the backbone.

3 Retrace the cut
Using long, smooth strokes, retrace the cut along the top side of backbone with the tip of the knife to free the top part of the fillet. Proceed slowly and methodically, holding the top of the fillet away from the cut as you go.

4 Remove the first fillet
Lift up the edge of the flesh to reveal the ribs. Continue to cut the flesh away, sliding the knife along the curve of the ribs to remove as much flesh as possible. Remove the first fillet and set it aside.

5 Cut the second fillet
Turn the fish over and make another crosswise diagonal cut to separate the flesh from the head. Again, cut along the top side of the backbone to free the top part of the second fillet.

6 Remove the second fillet
Cut the flesh away from the bones as with the first fillet, sliding the knife along the ribs. Remove the second fillet and set it aside. Reserve the bones from lean fish, if desired, for making stock or fumet (page 138).

Skinning a Fillet

1 Hold the skin securely

Position the tail end of a fillet near the edge of a dry cutting board. Holding the end of the tail with one hand, use a fillet knife or other long, slim-bladed knife to cut straight down to, but not through, the skin.

2 Slide the knife under the fillet

Holding the skin taut with one hand, position the blade at a slight angle upward between the skin and the flesh. Slide the blade back and forth along the skin, as if "shaving" off the flesh.

Pulling Out Pin Bones

1 Feel for bones

Lay a fillet, skin(ned) side down, on a board. Run a fingertip near the center from the thicker end toward the tail. If you feel the tips of bones sticking up, the pin bones are still in place.

2 Pull out the bones

Using fish tweezers or impeccably clean needle-nose pliers, pull out the bones one by one, gripping the tip of each bone and pulling up diagonally. This method will preserve the shape of whole fillets.

Cutting Out Pin Bones

1 Cut along the sides of the bones

The pin bones of some fish are easier to remove with a knife. Lay a fillet skin(ned) side down on a board. Using a boning or fillet knife, cut along one side of the pin bones and then the other.

2 Pull out the strip and bones

Using your fingers, pull out the thin strip of flesh containing the bones and discard. This method works well for flat fish, whose bones are sometimes difficult to access through other methods.

Portioning Large Fish Fillets

1 Note the fillet's angle
Look at the thick end of the fillet, which will probably be cut at an angle. Lay your knife against this cut edge and note the angle of the blade. You'll want to hold the knife at this same angle as you cut.

2 Cut the fillet in half by weight
Estimate the halfway point of the fillet, bearing in mind the weight difference due to the tapering shape. Holding the knife at the same angle as the fillet end, cut the fillet into 2 pieces of about equal weight.

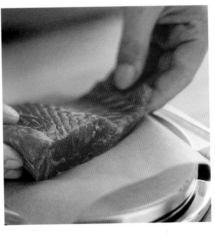

3 Cut the fillet into portions
Divide each fillet half into serving-sized portions (typically 4–6 oz/125–185 g each) according to your recipe and following the angle of the initial cut. The cuts may need to be farther apart as you approach the tail.

4 Weigh the portions for accuracy
Done correctly, you should have all of the fillet pieces roughly equal in weight, which will cook in the same amount of time. Use a kitchen scale, if desired, to test your accuracy as you cut.

SEAFOOD SAFETY

Seafood has generated more than its share of news stories about food-borne toxins and diseases. However, on a per-meal basis, fish and shellfish cause fewer illnesses than any other source of animal protein. Here are some tips for selecting seafood.

First, buy from reputable retailers. They will have information about the conditions of the waters where their fish and shellfish lived.

Second, eat from varied sources. Some fish naturally accumulate mercury, and some waters are more polluted than others.

Third, educate yourself. If you eat wild fish, check with local authorities for any advisories.

Finally, practice good shopping and storing habits. Use your eyes and nose when you're shopping to help you discern freshness. All fish should look moist and bright and have a fresh, clean scent. Be wary of even the slightest "off" aroma.

Refrigerate fresh fish the moment you bring it home from the store, and, ideally, cook it the day you buy it. To keep fresh fish in the optimum condition for use the following day, refrigerate the wrapped package in a baking pan, or any container large enough to hold it, and cover it with ice. Be sure the ice does not come into direct contact with the fish.

Creating a Parchment Packet for Steaming Fish

1 Create the packets

Cut out a 12-by-15-inch (30-by-38-cm) piece of parchment paper. Lay the paper on a work surface with the long edge facing you, and fold it in half like a book. Crease about 1 inch (2.5 cm) on the two ends of the fold.

2 Place the fish on the paper

Cut about 2 inches (5 cm) off the opposite open corners. Open the parchment and lay a fillet, skinned side down, about 1 inch (2.5 cm) to one side of the fold. Top with other ingredients as called for in your recipe.

3 Enclose the fish

Working with 1 packet at a time, fold the paper back over the fish, matching the edges. Starting at the end of the fold nearest you, fold the corner of the parchment in, creating a new corner.

4 Make a series of folds

Fold the new corner in toward the center and crease again, creating another new corner. Continue folding in this manner all the way around the packet, creative a curved border that encloses the fish.

5 Seal the packet

Reaching the other end, twist the end of the paper to seal the packet. Press the creases again to ensure that the steam remains inside the packet to cook the fish. Lay the packets on a rimmed baking sheet.

6 Test the fish for doneness

To test the fish, insert a wooden skewer through the paper into the thickest part of the fish, leave it there for a few seconds, then remove it and quickly touch it to your lower lip. If it is quite warm, the fish is done.

Peeling & Deveining Shrimp

1 Pull off the head and legs
Working with one shrimp at a time, grasp the head (if still on the shrimp) in one hand and the tail in the other and twist them apart. Then, pull off the small legs on the underside of the shrimp.

2 Pull the shell from the meat
Starting with the section of shell closest to the head, pull it up and lift it away. As you pull away the first section of shell, it will bring the other overlapping shell sections away with it.

3 Remove the final shell section
In some recipes, you can choose whether or not to pull off the final shell section, or "tail feathers." To do so, give the tip of the tail a squeeze as you pull, keeping the meat intact as you remove the shell.

4 Cut a shallow groove
Using a paring knife, make a shallow cut along the outer curve almost to the tail of each shrimp. You'll likely see a dark, veinlike intestinal tract running from head to tail through the meat.

5 Remove the vein
With the tip of the knife, lift out the vein and pull it away, gently scraping it with the knife if necessary. Place the shrimp in a colander and rinse with cold water to remove any residual grit.

TROUBLESHOOTING
Most shrimp have been frozen, and salting them heavily for a brief time once they are thawed improves their flavor and texture. Sprinkle with salt, let stand for no longer than 1 minute, then rinse with cold water.

Cleaning Mussels

1 Scrub the mussels
Using a stiff brush, scrub the mussels shells well under running cold water. Rinse away any mud, sand, or other shell grit. Discard any open mussels that do not close to the touch; these mollusks are dead.

2 Debeard the mussels
Locate the beard (the little fibrous tufts the mussel used to connect to rocks or pilings), if present, on the side of each mussel and scrape or cut it away with a paring knife or kitchen scissors.

3 Rinse the mussels
Gently place the mussels in a colander and give them a final rinse before using them. If you are not cooking them right away, place the mussels in a bowl set over ice for up to 24 hours.

4 Inspect the mollusks
Carefully examine each mussel for cracked or broken shells, a sign that the mussel is dead and must be discarded. Just before cooking, check again for shells that do not close to the touch.

Trimming Scallops

1 Locate the dense muscle strip
Look on the shorter side of the scallop to locate the strip of smaller, denser, more opaque meat. This strip of muscle cooks up tough, so for tender scallops, you'll want to remove it.

2 Remove the dense muscle strip
Using your fingers or a paring knife, pull or cut away the small muscle. The trimmings can be used along with fish bones and pieces to make stock or fumet (page 138) or they can be discarded.

Shucking Oysters

1 Scrub the oysters
Using a stiff brush, scrub the oyster shells well under running cold water. Rinse away any mud, sand, or other shell grit. Discard any open oysters that do not close to the touch; these mollusks are dead.

2 Grasp an oyster
Place a cleaned oyster on a work surface and identify the flat side. Fold a kitchen towel and use it to pick up the oyster so the flat side is facing up. The towel will protect your hand as you shuck.

3 Insert the oyster knife
Locate the hinge at the pointed end of the oyster. Insert the tip of an oyster knife about ½ inch (12 mm) deep into the hinge. Twist and pry the knife to loosen the top shell and break the hinge.

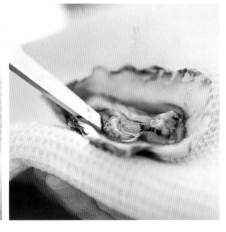

4 Detach the muscle
If the tip of the knife is muddy, rinse it in a bowl of water and wipe it clean. Slide the knife along the inside surface of the top shell to detach the adductor muscle that connects the oyster to the shell.

5 Remove the top shell
Now that you have severed the adductor muscle, the top shell should be free. Lift it away and discard. Be careful not to spill any of the juice, or oyster liquor in which the oyster sits inside the shell.

6 Loosen the oyster
Carefully run the knife along the inside surface of the bottom shell to loosen the oyster. Leave the oyster in the shell with its juice if serving on the half shell or pour the oyster with its liquor into a bowl.

Shucking Clams

1 Scrub the clams
Using a stiff brush, scrub the clams well under running cold water. Rinse away any mud, sand, or other shell grit. Discard any open clams that do not close to the touch. Hold a clam flat in the palm of one hand.

2 Insert the knife
Lay the edge of a clam knife against the seam between the shells. Wrap the fingers of the hand holding the clam around the back of the blade and gently squeeze until the blade slips into the shell.

3 Cut the first adductor muscle
Pull the knife almost out of the shell, then work the tip up against the upper shell to cut the adductor muscle on the far side. (Clams have two adductor muscles, near the opposite ends.)

4 Cut the second adductor muscle
Keeping the tip in the shell, slide the knife around toward the near side, loosening the meat and finally, cutting the remaining adductor muscle. Take care to preserve the clam liquor inside the shell.

5 Remove the top shell
Bend back the top shell and break it free. Run the knife along the inside surface of the bottom shell to loosen the clam. Leave the clam in the shell if serving on the half shell or pour the clam and juice into a bowl.

6 Inspect the mollusks
When buying and cleaning clams, check them over for any open shells. If their shells do not quickly shut tight after prodding, discard them or pass them by. Shells that won't close indicate the clam is dead.

Cleaning Squid

1 Separate the tentacles
Place the squid on a cutting board. Using a chef's knife, cut off the tentacles just below the eyes of the squid. Be careful not to cut too far away from the eyes or the tentacles will fall apart.

2 Remove the beak
Pick up the tentacle portion and firmly squeeze the cut end of the tentacles to expose the hard, round "beak" at the base. Pull out and discard the beak. Set the tentacles aside.

3 Remove the head and innards
Gently squeezing the mantle, or tube-like body, of the squid, pull away the head. The entrails, including the ink sac, should come away with the head. Discard the head and the attached entrails.

4 Remove the quill
Reach into the mantle and pull out the long, transparent, plasticlike quill along with any remaining entrails and discard. Thoroughly rinse the mantle and tentacles under cold running water.

5 Skin the squid
If desired, pull off the skin from the mantle, using a paring knife to help scrape it away if necessary. If left in place, the skin will give the cooked squid a pinkish cast and a bit more texture.

6 Cut the body into rings
If directed, cut the mantle into rings about ⅜ inch (1 cm) wide. Put the rings in a large bowl of cold water, swish them around to thoroughly rinse away any loose bits, and then drain.

Boiling & Cleaning Crabs

1 Boil the crabs
Fill a stockpot with about 8 qt (8 l) cool water and ¼ cup (1¼ oz/37 g) kosher salt. Pick up the crab from behind and immerse it in the water. Cover the pot and bring to a full boil, then turn off the heat.

2 Let the crabs steep
Let blue crabs steep in the hot water for about 10 minutes, Dungeness, about 15, until the shells turn bright red. Using long tongs, lift the crab from the water, turning it over the pot to drain away any water.

3 Remove the apron
Transfer the crabs to a cutting board. For a Dungeness crab, place it shell side down on a board and lift off and discard the triangular tail flap, or apron. Watch out for the spines on the underside, which are sharp.

4 Remove the top shell
Turn the crab. Holding it by the legs, lift off and discard the hard top shell. If desired, scoop out and reserve the pale yellow crab fat in the shell. Blue and Dungeness crabs can be cleaned in this same way.

5 Remove the gills and intestines
Next, pull off and discard the grayish, feathery gills that lie along both sides of the crab body, the jaw section at the front, and the intestines in the middle. Wipe up any mess on the board. Rinse the body well.

6 Pick out the meat
Twist the claws and legs from the body. Using a large chef's knife or your hands, cut or break the body into halves lengthwise along its center and then into quarters. Use a seafood fork to extract the meat from the shells.

Eyeing Doneness

1 Cut into the fish

Using the tip of a paring knife, cut into the flesh of the fish in an area that won't mar its appearance when serving. Unless you are cooking fish to the rare stage, the interior should be barely opaque but still moist.

TROUBLESHOOTING

Overcooked fish will look dry, be very firm, and will flake apart when you cut into it. To prevent overcooking, test for doneness periodically. A general rule is to cook fish for 10 minutes per inch of thickness.

Other Doneness Tests

1 Test the fish by temperature

Insert an instant-read thermometer into the thickest part of a fish (usually near the head on a whole fish), but don't go through the meat into the cavity. Most fish are done when they reach 115°–125°F (46–52°C).

2 Test the fish by feel

Insert a wooden skewer or wire cake tester into the thickest part of the fish. It should enter easily with little resistance. Or, touch the skewer to your lower lip; when done, the skewer will feel quite warm.

TESTING FISH FOR DONENESS

One rule applies to every method of cooking seafood, from grilling to roasting to frying: Don't overcook it.

By Sight Most fish is done when it is opaque throughout, and when the fish is prodded with a fork the juices should run milky white. The two exceptions are salmon, which is best cooked only until it is still translucent in the center, and ahi tuna, which is usually cooked only until rare or medium-rare.

By Temperature An instant-read thermometer is useful for checking whole fish, thicker steaks, and other large cuts. Fish protein firms up at a lower temperature than other meats, and most types are fully cooked when they reach 115° (46°) to 125°F (52°C). Cook them any further and they will be tough and dry.

By Feel For thinner pieces, insert a knife or skewer in the center and feel for resistance (try it first on the raw fish to get a feel for the difference). When the point slips in and out with little "grip," the fish is done.

Testing Shellfish Bivalves are ready when their shells open wide (discard any that fail to open during cooking), and shrimp should be cooked just until opaque; looking into the groove left by deveining, if present, can help you confirm that they are done. Crab and lobster are done when their shells turn bright red.

Using a Chimney Starter

1 Stuff the chimney starter
A chimney starter is an easy way to start a charcoal fire without imparting unwanted flavors to your food. Remove the grill grate. Upend the chimney starter on the fire bed and stuff loosely with newspaper.

2 Add the coals
Remove the cooking grate from the grill and turn the chimney starter right side up on the fire bed, keeping the newspaper secure in the bottom. Add briquettes or hardwood charcoal to the top of the canister.

3 Ignite the newspaper
Using a gas wand or long-handled match, light the newspaper. The flames will rise upward and ignite the coals. Let the coals burn in the chimney starter until covered with a layer of white ash.

TROUBLESHOOTING
If the newspaper is packed too firmly in the chimney, it will hinder the oxygen flow and prevent the paper from lighting. You should only need 2–3 full sheets of crumpled paper. Remove some as needed and restart the fire.

Direct-heat Fire

1 Pour the ignited coals
When the coals in the chimney starter are covered with a layer of white ash, protect your hand and arm with a grill mitt, turn the chimney starter over, and dump the coals into the fire bed.

2 Arrange the coals
Using long-handled tongs, arrange the coals 2–3 layers deep in one-third of the fire bed and 1–2 layers deep in another third, leaving the remaining third free of coals. Move food to the cool part to control flare-ups.

Indirect-heat Fire

1 Arrange the coals on two sides

After pouring the coals into the fire bed (see left), use long-handled tongs to arrange the coals in 2 equal piles on 2 sides of the grill, leaving a wide area in the center of the fire bed free of coals.

2 Position a drip pan

Place an aluminum-foil pan in the area in the center of the coals to catch the dripping fat and create a cool zone for the grill. To control smoke, add enough water to fill the pan halfway up the sides.

Using Wood Chips

1 Soak the wood chips

Soak hardwood chips, such as mesquite, hickory, or cherry, in a large bowl with water to cover. Let soak for at least 30 minutes. The wet chips will smolder on the fire, producing a good head of smoke.

2 Add the wood chips

For a charcoal grill, sprinkle a handful of soaked wood chips directly onto the hot coals. For a gas grill, add the wood chips to a smoker box according to the manufacturer's directions.

Oiling the Grill Grate

1 Dip rolled paper towels in oil

Pour a moderate amount of canola oil into a small container. Fold a stack of 4 paper towels in half, then roll them up tightly into a cylinder. Using tongs, grasp the towel roll and soak it in the oil.

2 Rub the grate with the oil

Still using the tongs, brush the grill grate with the oiled towels. The oil keeps food, particularly fish and other delicate items, from sticking to the grill grate and makes cleanup easier.

Serving & Garnishing

Once you have shopped for, prepared, and cooked your fish to perfection, it deserves some attention when you serve it. Showcase your efforts by selecting the right serving dishes and adding a simple garnish.

Whether you decide to serve your seafood meal family-style on a platter or on individual plates, or garnished with a drizzle of sauce or a sprig of fresh herbs, follow these tips to ensure that everything stays fresh and delicious and looks the best it can by the time you bring it to the table.

Keep in mind the tone you wish to set for your meal. For an elegant dinner party, you may want to plate individual portions. On the other hand, for a more casual or informal meal, you may want to serve the food family-style from a large platter, letting guests serve themselves.

Different dishes inspire different levels of formality, so follow your instincts and consider what best complements your dish or the company. If you are serving seafood in shells, such as clams or mussels, remember to set out additional bowls for diners to discard the empty shells.

A simple garnish can add both color and variety to any plate. Any garnish that you choose should be edible, and ideally should relate to the flavors in the dish.

If a recipe calls for herbs, consider using one of the herbs as a garnish, either a few sprigs to adorn a serving platter, or finely chopped

and scattered on top of individual dishes. Lemon wedges or slices are a traditional garnish for fish and seafood dishes, and have the added appeal in that they can be used by diners to season their food to taste. If serving on a platter, consider surrounding the seafood with a side dish, such as roasted potatoes or serving it atop a bed of colorful rice pilaf flecked with fresh herbs. Finally, crisp, fresh lettuce leaves or sprigs of fresh herbs are a simple and pretty way to make a colorful bed for almost any cold seafood dish.

Delicate fish and shellfish cools relatively quickly once it is plated and served, so you may want to gently warm the serving dishes ahead of time, to help keep your creations as warm and appealing as possible.

Warm individual plates and serving platters in a low (200°F/95°C) oven for about 15 minutes before the recipe is ready. If you are already using your oven for broiling or roasting, place the plates on top of the oven to warm them. Make sure to use oven mitts when removing the plates from the oven in case they are too hot to the touch.

Likewise, cold dishes such as seafood salads taste best when they are served on chilled dishes. Place the dishes in the refrigerator at least 10 minutes prior to serving.

Carving a Whole Fish

1 Transfer to a serving platter
Whole fish can be presented on a serving platter or served directly from the cooking vessel. To transfer the fish to a serving platter, use a spatula and large spoon to ease it onto the platter.

2 Cut through the skin
Using the edge of a large metal serving spoon, cut through the skin lengthwise along the dorsal fin on the upper side of the fish. Use a second spoon in your other hand to steady the fish as you cut.

3 Remove the first fillet
Slide the bottom spoon against the bones and toward the ribs as you lift away a portion of the flesh and skin, using the other spoon to steady it from the top. For large fish, you may need to do this in pieces.

4 Remove the backbone
Once all the flesh on the top fillet is removed, slide a spoon under the backbone and lift it away. This gives you access to the second fillet underneath. Use the spoon(s) to transfer the bottom fillet to the platter or board.

ROUNDING OUT THE MEAL

Here are a few easy ideas for accompaniments to complement your delicious fish dinners.

Tomato salad Slice fresh, ripe tomatoes and season with olive oil, salt, and pepper. If desired, add feta cheese, olives, or fresh herbs.

Garlic bread Halve a ciabatta loaf lengthwise and brush with minced garlic and butter. Toast under the broiler, taking care is doesn't burn.

Roasted red potatoes Scrub and halve baby red potatoes, then toss them in a little olive oil, salt, and pepper. Roast in a single layer on a baking sheet at 425°F (220°C) for 15–20 minutes, stirring occasionally.

Steamed asparagus In a steamer basket set in a saucepan over simmering water, steam trimmed asparagus spears until tender-crisp, 5–7 minutes. Toss with butter or olive oil and season to taste.

Roasted vegetables Toss vegetables, such as broccoli or cauliflower florets, summer squash, or asparagus in olive oil. Roast in a single layer on a baking sheet at 425°F (220°C) until tender-crisp, 7–10 minutes. Season the vegetables to taste.

Couscous Cook instant couscous according to package directions. Before serving, fluff the grains with a fork and stir in chopped toasted almonds or fresh herbs to taste.

Basic Recipes

The following pages offer some staple recipes for stocks, sauces, and accompaniments that are called for throughout the book, but which are also useful additions to any cook's repertoire.

Fish Stock

1½ lb (750 g) fish heads and/or bones from white-fleshed, nonoily fish such as snapper, flounder, or halibut, well rinsed

1 large yellow onion, coarsely chopped

½ fennel bulb, coarsely chopped

3 celery stalks, coarsely chopped

1 carrot, peeled and diced

1 leek, including tender green parts, chopped

2 cups (16 fl oz/500 ml) dry white wine

In a large saucepan, combine the fish parts, onion, fennel, celery, carrot, leek, 6 cups (48 fl oz/1.5 l) water, and the wine. Place over medium heat and bring gradually to a boil, skimming off foam as needed. Cover partially, reduce the heat to low, and simmer until the flesh starts to fall off the bones, about 40 minutes.

Line a sieve with cheesecloth and place over a clean container. Strain the stock through the sieve. Use at once or let cool, cover tightly, and refrigerate for up to 3 days or freeze for up to 3 months.

MAKES ABOUT 2 QT (2 L)

Fish Fumet

1 tbsp canola oil

1 large leek, white and pale green parts only, sliced

1 stalk celery, roughly chopped

1½ lb (750 g) fish heads and/or bones from white-fleshed, nonoily fish such as snapper, flounder, or halibut, well rinsed

3 sprigs fresh flat-leaf parsley

8 peppercorns

2 sprigs fresh thyme

¼ tsp fennel seeds

½ bay leaf

¾ cup (6 fl oz/180 ml) dry white wine

Place a Dutch oven or a large saucepan with a lid over low to medium-low heat and add the oil. When hot, add the leek and celery and cover the pot. Cook, stirring occasionally, until the vegetables soften without browning, about 5 minutes.

Add the fish heads and/or bones, the wine, and water to cover the ingredients by about 1 inch (2.5 cm), and raise the heat to high. As soon as you see bubbles forming, reduce the heat to low. Skim off any foam that rises to the top, then add the parsley, peppercorns, thyme, fennel seeds, and bay leaf. Reduce the heat to low and simmer, regularly skimming any foam on the surface, until the fumet is full flavored, about 20 minutes. Add additional water, if necessary, to keep the ingredients just submerged and watch that the fumet doesn't come to a boil.

Carefully pour the fumet through a sieve lined with damp cheesecloth into a large heatproof bowl. Use the fumet at once, or cool and store it. Cover and refrigerate for up to 2 days or pour into airtight containers and freeze for up to 2 months.

MAKES ABOUT 6 CUPS (48 FL OZ/1.5 L)

Clarified Butter

½ cup (4 oz/125 g) unsalted butter

In a small saucepan over low heat, melt the butter. When the butter is melted, remove the pan from the heat and let stand for about 2 minutes.

Using a large metal spoon, skim the foam and solids from the surface of the butter and discard them; these are impurities that have risen to the top. Carefully pour the clear yellow liquid into a heatproof measuring cup, leaving behind the white milk solids in the bottom of the saucepan.

MAKES ABOUT ⅓ CUP (3 FL OZ/80 ML)

Roasted Peppers

2 red and/or yellow bell peppers

Position the oven rack as close to the heat source as possible and preheat the broiler. Arrange the peppers on a rimmed baking sheet lined with aluminum foil.

Place the peppers under the broiler and cook, turning as needed with tongs, until charred and blistered on all sides, about 15 minutes.

Transfer the roasted peppers to a paper bag, close the bag loosely, and set aside to cool. Remove the cooled peppers from the bag and use your fingers to peel and rub away as much of the charred skin as possible. Cut the peppers in half lengthwise and cut or pull out the stems, seeds, and ribs.

MAKES 2 ROASTED PEPPERS

Tomatillo Salsa

12 oz (375 g) tomatillos, husked and rinsed

2 serrano chiles

½ cup chopped fresh cilantro

½ cup (2½ oz/75 g) chopped onion

4 cloves garlic

2 tbsp fresh lime juice

2 tbsp cider vinegar

1 tsp sugar

Kosher salt and freshly ground pepper

Preheat the broiler. Spread the tomatillos and chiles on a rimmed baking sheet and broil until browned and blackened in spots, about 15 minutes. Let cool.

Transfer the tomatillos and chiles to a blender along with the cilantro, onion, garlic, lime juice, vinegar, sugar, ½ teaspoon salt and ¼ cup (2 fl oz/60 ml) water and blend until a smooth purée forms. Pour into a bowl and season to taste.

MAKES ABOUT 2 CUPS (16 FL OZ/500 ML)

Creamy Polenta

Kosher salt and freshly ground pepper

1½ cups (7½ oz/235 g) polenta

3 tbsp unsalted butter

½ cup (6 oz/188 g) freshly grated Parmesan cheese

In a large heavy pot over high heat, bring 6 cups water to a boil with 1½ teaspoons salt. Whisking constantly, add the polenta in a thin stream. Reduce the heat to medium and cook, whisking for 2 minutes, until the polenta has begun to thicken. Reduce the heat to low and simmer, covered, until the polenta thickens and pulls away from the sides of the pan, 45 minutes. Stir the polenta for 1 minute after every 10 minutes of cooking.

Remove the polenta from heat and stir in the butter and cheese. Serve right away.

MAKES 4 SERVINGS

Mayonnaise

1 large egg yolk

1 tsp Dijon mustard

Pinch of coarse salt

¾ cup olive oil

Pinch of freshly ground pepper

1 tsp lemon juice, or to taste

In a bowl, combine the egg yolk, mustard, and salt. Whisk together. Very gradually whisk in the olive oil, a drop at a time, until the mixture begins to thicken. Continue whisking and pouring in the remaining oil in a thin stream until very thick and opaque in color. Stir in the pepper and lemon juice,

or to taste. Store in a covered jar in the refrigerator for up to 1 week.

MAKES ABOUT 1 CUP (8 FL OZ/250 ML)

Variation: Aioli

Stir 2 cloves garlic, pressed with a garlic press, into the finished mayonnaise.

Variation: Tartar Sauce

Stir 1 tbsp minced sweet or dill pickles, 1 tbsp minced capers, and 1 tbsp minced shallot into the finished mayonnaise.

Rouille

½ cup (3 oz/90 g) roasted red pepper pieces

1 cup (5 oz/155 g) cooked, peeled, diced red potatoes

4 cloves garlic, minced

1 tsp kosher salt

½ tsp red pepper flakes

½ cup (4 fl oz/125 ml) extra-virgin olive oil

In a food processor, combine the bell pepper, potatoes, garlic, salt, and pepper flakes and process until smooth. With the motor running, slowly add the olive oil in a thin, steady stream until incorporated. Transfer to a bowl and refrigerate until serving time.

MAKES ABOUT 2 CUPS (16 FL OZ/500 ML)

Index